Power Plays

POWER PLAYS

by
Elaine May
and
Alan Arkin

Garden City, New York

Elaine May and Alan Arkin's POWER PLAYS premiered on March 12, 1998, at A Contemporary Theater in Seattle. It opened at the Manhattan Theatre Club in New York City on May 21, 1998. It was produced by Julian Schlossberg, Meyer Ackerman, Ben Sprecher, William P. Miller and the Manhattan Theatre Club. It was directed by Alan Arkin. Set design was by Michael McGarty, costumes design was by Michael Krass, wig and hair design was by Paul Huntley, lighting design was by Adam Silverman and sound design was by Andrew S. Keister. Company manager was Rise' Jablonka. Production stage manager was Deidre McCrane. Assistant stage manager was David A. Winitsky. General management was provided by Soloway/Levy. Press representative was Boneau/Bryan-Brown.

THE CAST
(In Order of Appearance)

Elaine May
Alan Arkin
Jeannie Berlin
Anthony Arkin

The Way
of
All Fish

by
Elaine May

An office, richly furnished: wood paneling, suede sofa, Persian rugs. Ms. Asquith, perfectly groomed and expensively dressed, sits behind an impressive desk. Miss Riverton, her secretary, much less expensively dressed, stands in front of her.

Ms. Asquith: Miss Riverton.

Miss Riverton: Yes?

Ms. Asquith: Do you remember my distinctly telling you that I wanted nothing thrown out?

Miss Riverton: Yes.

Ms. Asquith: Well, you've thrown out my exercise elastic.

Miss Riverton: Oh, I don't think so.

Ms. Asquith: Well, here it is—in the wastebasket and I didn't put it there.

Miss Riverton: Oh, is *that* your . . . Oh, forgive me. I thought it was a piece of old rubber.

Ms. Asquith: It doesn't *matter* what you thought it was. The point is—you threw it out.

Miss Riverton: Well, yes . . . because I thought it was rubbish.

Ms. Asquith: Miss Riverton, I didn't ask you to use your best judgment. I didn't say, "Throw out what you think is rubbish and keep the rest." I said, "Don't throw anything out."

Miss Riverton: Well . . . but what about rubbish?

Ms. Asquith: Rubbish is not your affair. I have a maid who deals with rubbish.

Miss Riverton: Yes, I see.

Ms. Asquith: Your job is to see that my life runs smoothly and my appointments are kept. You are my secretary—not my housekeeper.

Miss Riverton: Assistant. Yes, of course.

Ms. Asquith: You are not my assistant, Miss Riverton. You are my secretary.

Miss Riverton: Alright.

Ms. Asquith: I don't like to call something something else just because it's politically correct. A secretary is a perfectly fine thing to be.

Miss Riverton: But I do assist you.

Ms. Asquith: Yes, you do. And so does a secretary.

Miss Riverton: But . . . isn't an assistant closer to what I do?

Ms. Asquith: No, it isn't. It just uses the verb assist as a noun. You don't assist me in altering my clothes or cutting my hair or doing my nails. You assist me in the way a secretary does, a word, which you may be interested to know, originally meant "desk."

Miss Riverton: Yes, I see.

Ms. Asquith: Thank you. That will be all. (*She rises, goes out, comes back*) Where am I going?

Miss Riverton: When?

Ms. Asquith: Now.

Misss Riverton: Nowhere.

Ms. Asquith: Nowhere? That's impossible. It's Friday night.

Miss Riverton: Yes, I know.

Ms. Asquith: Well . . . how did this happen?

Miss Riverton: You had an engagement with Nelson Miles and then the Stradners invited you for a sail around East Hampton with Princess Agnelli and Ralph Lauren so you canceled Mr. Miles. Then the Stradners canceled because of the weather and it was too late to get Mr. Miles back so you placed a call to your son so you could invite him to dinner but he told me he was going out of town with his father and stepmother on a long weekend to visit her parents' dairy farm. Then it was today.

Ms. Asquith: You know, Miss Riverton, when you place a call for me, I would appreciate it if you didn't discuss the purpose of my call with the person I'm calling. You shouldn't have asked my son if he was free for dinner on Friday. I didn't ask you to do that.

Miss Riverton: Yes, but he said "what does she want?"

Ms. Asquith: It doesn't matter what he said. *You* should have said "one moment and I'll put her on."

Miss Riverton: You were on another call.

Ms. Asquith: It doesn't matter.

Miss Riverton: It's just that I thought you were busy.

Ms. Asquith: I was busy. I am busy. I'm a busy woman. But it still doesn't matter. My son lives in a dorm. It takes time to get him on the phone. Time you save me by instituting . . . I'm not going to be made to feel guilty because I don't personally dial every member of my family.

Miss Riverton: I assure you I had no intention of making you feel guilty.

Ms. Asquith: Well, I *am* guilty. So it doesn't take much.

Ms. Riverton: I'm sorry. It's just . . . (*She breaks off*)

Ms. Asquith: What?

Miss Riverton: Nothing, really. It's not important.

Ms. Asquith: Miss Riverton, please finish your sentence. It drives me crazy when you do that. What? I want to know. What? (*Miss Riverton shakes her head*) Oh, *don't* make me go through this. WHAT?

Miss Riverton: Well, it's just that your son . . . has said . . . a few times he's said . . . that . . . he's said that it's rude to call someone and then make them wait while you—not *you*, anyone—comes to the phone. It's like knocking at the door and then leaving a sign saying "Back in a minute—stay right there."

Ms. Asquith (*after a moment*): He's right.

Miss Riverton: He says no matter how fast someone gets there . . .

Ms. Asquith: No, no, no, he's right, he's absolutely right. I *do* do that. All the time. No wonder I'm guilty. Of course, it would just cut my day in half if I dialed all those numbers and then had to wait for a secretary to answer and tell me whether or not someone could come to the phone . . . and half the time they couldn't . . . and then I had to leave a message that I called . . .

Miss Riverton: Perhaps if you just did it with family and close friends . . .

Ms. Asquith: Yes. That's a good idea. Remind me to do that. Did he ask to talk to me? My son?

Miss Riverton: No. He said he knew you were busy.

Ms. Asquith (*she sighs*): What a lousy week.

Miss Riverton: It *has* been complicated.

Ms. Asquith: Awful. The worst. First the root canal and then this hideous haircut and then I got on the scale this morning and I'd gained three pounds— because I couldn't find my exercise elastic and I was just too irritated to work out. Thank God the mammogram turned out all right. I have to keep things in perspective.

Miss Riverton: I'm sorry about the elastic.

Ms. Asquith: Well . . . These things happen.

Miss Riverton: Tomorrow night is Lincoln Center. You've been looking forward to that.

Ms. Asquith: Tomorrow night is twenty-four hours away. (*After a moment*) What are *you* doing tonight, Miss Riverton?

Miss Riverton: Me? Nothing.

Ms. Asquith: Well . . . would you care to come home with me and have dinner?

Miss Riverton: Thank you, but . . . the cook and maid are off tonight.

Ms. Asquith: WHAT!

Miss Riverton: You told me . . .

Ms. Asquith: Oh, *no*!

Miss Riverton: . . . they wouldn't be needed because of the Stradner dinner party.

Ms. Asquith: But the Stradners canceled.

Miss Riverton: Yes, but they didn't cancel until Thursday night and I didn't get the message until this morning and by then the cook and the maid were gone.

Ms. Asquith: Oh, shit! It's just the fucking end of the world.

Miss Riverton: I'm sorry.

Ms. Asquith: Don't be silly. How could you know the Stradners would cancel.

Miss Riverton: I was thinking about the exercise elastic. It's so awful to gain weight.

Ms. Asquith: Forget the exercise elastic. The exercise elastic is past. The exercise elastic is just something to sustain me between sessions. The important thing is—what are we going to eat. (*Looks at her watch*) It's too late to get into a really decent restaurant. Even for me. Oh, *God*. Can we order in?

Miss Riverton: Yes. What would you like.

Ms. Asquith: I don't know. Pasta? Fish?

Miss Riverton: Perhaps Japanese. You like Japanese.

Ms. Asquith: Yes. Japanese would be good. Order Japanese. (*As Miss Riverton picks up the phone and dials*) Order something I like. But nothing raw.

Miss Riverton: Nothing raw.

Ms. Asquith: I'm afraid of parasites.

Miss Riverton: Well, would you like . . .

Ms. Asquith: Don't ask me what I'd like. I'm no good at that. You pick it.

Miss Riverton (*into phone*): Yes, I'd like to place an order—322 Madison Avenue . . .

Ms. Asquith: Order shumai . . .

Miss Riverton: . . . The penthouse . . .

Ms. Asquith: Ask if they have soft-shell-crab.

Miss Riverton: . . . Asquith Enterprises. Do you have soft-shell crab? . . .

Ms. Asquith: Roll. Hand roll.

Miss Riverton: One soft-shell crab roll, hand roll. One shumai . . .

Miss Riverton (*overlapping*): ... one California roll ... *two* shumai ... one Manhattan roll—*three* shumai ... and three soft-shell crab rolls. No that's two besides the last one. Three altogether. Two shrimp teriyaki. Another California roll and extra brown rice and saki. (*She hangs up*)

Ms. Asquith (*overlapping*): Maybe two shumai—but they're small ... three shumai ... and three soft-shell crab rolls ... and shrimp teriyaki. Did you tell him shrimp teriyaki? And maybe two California rolls ... no—yes—two. And rice, extra rice, brown rice and saki. Plenty of saki.

Ms. Asquith: Perfect. Oh, yum. Get some plates and we'll set the desk ... (*calling, as Miss Riverton runs off*) ... and I opened two excellent bottles of wine for lunch before that barbarian, Charles, said no alcohol—what assholes accountants are. Now ... Let's see—where's the wine ... the wine ... Ah! Here it is. And two glasses.

(*Miss Riverton comes back in carrying plates, napkins, and silverware and heads for the desk*)

Ms. Asquith (*as she pours the wine*): Oh, this is going to be such fun. Just like a picnic. Perhaps we should set the coffee table instead of the desk. More picnick-y.

(*Miss Riverton stops and heads for the coffee table*)

Ms. Asquith: But it's low.

(*Miss Riverton stops again*)

Ms. Asquith: Maybe the desk *is* better.

(*Miss Riverton heads back for the desk*)

Ms. Asquith: Oh, what if it *is* low. We'll sit on the floor. Here.

(*Miss Riverton heads back to the coffee table*)

Ms. Asquith (*holding out a glass*): Just put the plates down anywhere and try some of this.

Miss Riverton (*setting the plates on a chair*): Yes, Ms. Asquith.

Ms. Asquith: Perhaps you should call me Margaret for tonight. Well . . . perhaps not. (*Holds out a glass*) Well, what shall we drink to?

Miss Riverton: To your having a wonderful time at Lincoln Center tomorrow night.

Ms. Asquith: Lovely.

(*They clink glasses and sip*)

Miss Riverton: Oh, this *is* good.

Ms. Asquith: Isn't it? I'm glad you appreciate it. So many people have no understanding of wine.

Miss Riverton: I know. Long ago I made a pact with myself never to drink wine unless it was very, very good. This is excellent.

Ms. Asquith: Really. That's fascinating. How did you develop such an interest in wine?

Miss Riverton: My father was French.

Ms. Asquith: Ah. Enough said.

Miss Riverton: Oh, this is *very* good.

Ms. Asquith: Hmm. *So* good. Such clarity.

Miss Riverton: And subtlety. The wine presents itself but not boldly. Delicately, innocently.

Ms. Asquith: Well put. Very well put. (*Pouring more wine*) I guess I'll be having a few additional sessions with my trainer next week.

Miss Riverton: May I suggest . . .

(*She breaks off*)

Ms. Asquith: Yes? Oh, please. *Please* finish your sentence. It just drives me up the wall when you do that. This is a social evening. All the rules are changed. You just say whatever comes into your mind.

Miss Riverton: Well, all I was going to say is—I wonder if your trainer does quite enough aerobic work with you.

Ms. Asquith: You think I'm fat?

Miss Riverton: No, no. I'm just talking . . . health-wise, weight control-wise.

Ms. Asquith: He does half an hour.

Miss Riverton: Well . . . sometimes not a full half hour. And is a half hour on the trampoline enough?

Ms. Asquith: You don't approve of the trampoline?

Miss Riverton: Oh, I do. It's just that so much of the movement is momentum. Fast walking or jogging is much more effective.

Ms. Asquith: How do you know so much about this?

Miss Riverton: I'm very interested in the body.

Ms. Asquith: You're in wonderful shape.

Miss Riverton: Thank you. I'm very strong for a woman.

Ms. Asquith: You look very strong.

Miss Riverton: Too strong?

Ms. Asquith: Don't be silly. You can't look too strong. The appearance of strength is the appearance of power. Do you know the real difference between men and women, Miss Riverton? (*Miss Riverton shakes her head*) Strength. Sheer physical strength. Do you know that there are male fish that actually change sex when a bigger fish comes along because only the biggest fish can be male. All the rest of the fish are his harem.

Miss Riverton: You're joking.

Ms. Asquith: Absolutely not. And these fish have it down to such a science they don't even have to fight—they just measure. The fish that seems most likely to inflict injury wins.

Miss Riverton: Well, it's . . . it's certainly . . . certainly a man's world if you're a fish, isn't it?

Ms. Asquith: That's not my point, Miss Riverton. My point is that it's not whether you're a man or a woman that determines who's world it is, it's how strong you are that determines whether you're a man or a woman. Metaphorically, of course.

Miss Riverton: Of course. I see. Well . . . I'm very strong.

Ms. Asquith: Yes, I've seen you carry those file boxes. (*Pours more wine*) You know, Miss Riverton—Jane—you're the best secretary I've ever had. I can't tell you the idiots I had to put up with until you came along. I don't think I could get along without you, Jane.

Miss Riverton: Joan. Well . . . thank you. I try to do my job.

Ms. Asquith: Joan? Oh, what a fool I am.

Miss Riverton: No, no, no.

Ms. Asquith: This is so embarrassing.

Miss Riverton: Not at all.

Ms. Asquith: To have had you as my secretary for so long and not know your first name.

Miss Riverton: Well, you don't call me by my first name. And you were very close. Jane . . . Joan.

Ms. Asquith: I'll bet you know my first name.

Miss Riverton: Well, yes. But I make out all your checks and handle your mail.

Ms. Asquith: There's that. But no—that's the easy way out. I don't know your first name because I don't notice anything. That's a terrible failing of mine. I don't really notice people unless they're directly in my line of vision, part of what I'm focusing on. That was one of the reasons for my divorce. One day I handed my husband an envelope and said "Mail this for me." And he said "Can't your secretary mail it?" and I said "Oh, I'm sorry, darling. I didn't realize I was talking to you."

Miss Riverton: That doesn't seem so awful . . . I mean, awful enough for a divorce.

Ms. Asquith: Well—it wasn't just that . . . that discussion. It turned out he'd been very miserable for a very long time. But, of course, I didn't notice. I'm very insensitive. And everyone has to forgive me. Until they don't.

Miss Riverton: I think you're wonderful.

Ms. Asquith: Well . . . thank you, Joan. But it's a shortcoming—being blind to others. Power in a relationship belongs to whoever wants to leave first— and you can't anticipate that unless you notice the other person. The irony is that I wondered for years if I didn't make a mistake marrying him, if I couldn't have done better, if it wasn't a waste of my time—all those vacations, and dinners, and preludes to sex. And the minute he said he wanted a divorce I realized that I loved him madly. Madly. And it was too late.

(*There is a brief pause*)

Miss Riverton: Shall I get the other bottle of wine?

Ms. Asquith: Yes. Thank you. (*Watching Miss Riverton rise*) You know, Joan, I'm having just a wonderful time. I'm *glad* the Stradner's canceled.

Miss Riverton: This is very pleasant.

Ms. Asquith: So you're from France.

Miss Riverton: No. I'm from Michigan. My father was from France.

Ms. Asquith: Michigan! I've heard so much about Michigan. We always went to Italy or the South of France. But I wish we'd gone to Michigan. It sounds lovely.

Miss Riverton: And I wish we'd gone to the South of France. Life is funny.

Ms. Asquith: Very.

(*Miss Riverton pulls the cork out of the second wine bottle with a pop*)

Miss Riverton: Good sound. That's very important. My father taught me that. He was a room service waiter in Cannes. He started the same year as the film festival.

Ms. Asquith: How interesting.

Miss Riverton: It was all before I was born, of course.

Ms. Asquith: Of course. That's when everything interesting happens.

Miss Riverton: But seeing the south of France and Italy . . . that must have been interesting . . .

Ms. Asquith: It wasn't. Not to me. I'll tell you a secret that no one else knows. I was a fat child.

Miss Riverton: No!

Ms. Asquith: And a fat teenager. I went to school in Switzerland and Swiss food is just butter looking for a reason. By the time I was thirteen I was so fat they called me petite vache yanquee.

Miss Riverton: Petite vache yanquee?

Ms. Asquith: "Little yankee cow." Switzerland can be very cruel.

Miss Riverton: Oh, Miss Asquith—underneath everything I think you're a very vulnerable woman.

Ms. Asquith: Well, I'm not. I can't tell you how much I hate that word. I have no idea why everyone thinks it's so special to be vulnerable. It's a self-pitying, time-consuming preoccupation and everyone has it. Hitler was vulnerable. He sobbed on Mother's Day. What does that tell you?

Miss Riverton: I didn't know that about Hitler. Well, that changes things. I always thought he was just this awful man.

(*Ms. Asquith stares at her . . . then laughs*)

Ms. Asquith: Very good. I must remember that. (*Slugging back her wine*) So tell me more about Michigan.

Miss Riverton: Well, there's not a whole lot more to tell. It was very cold. In the winter. And then in the summer it got hot. Not a good climate.

Ms. Asquith: No. (*She pours more wine*) So you came to New York.

Miss Riverton: Yes. That's right.

Ms. Asquith: Wonderful story. Well, I can tell you I'm hungry.

Miss Riverton: It's a pretty boring story.

Ms. Asquith: No, no. Not at all.

Miss Riverton: I've had a pretty boring life.

Ms. Asquith: Nonsense. With a father who worked in Cannes and traveling from Michigan to New York . . .

Miss Riverton: When I was young I so wanted to be someone special.

Ms. Asquith: Well, you are someone special.

Miss Riverton: I mean, you know, someone, special, who everyone knows is special. I guess what I'm saying is I wanted to be famous.

Ms. Asquith: Ah, well.

Miss Riverton: Because being famous is . . . like being immortal, isn't it?

Ms. Asquith: Well—only if you're very famous for a very long time.

Miss Riverton: But you can be. Anyone can be. And
I know how. You know how? You can kill someone
famous. Of course, it has to be someone *really* famous and people have to be convinced that you're
not part of a conspiracy. And meeting someone famous isn't so easy. When I was younger that's all I
thought about—who can I kill who's famous and
how can I meet him. Probably I should have been
thinking how can I meet who's famous and how can
I kill him—but I was just a kid. (*She pours some
wine*) I thought of killing the President but everyone who tries to kill the President is such a slug. I
mean, I made a list of successful presidential assas-
sins who still had some kind of stature and you
know who there is? Booth. Because he killed
Lincoln. And where are you going to find another
Lincoln? And—I don't know—it just seems like
such a failure of imagination to go right to the
President: kill someone famous—kill the President.
Duh. Of course, Jack the Ripper is still famous and
he just killed a lot of totally unknown prostitutes.
But that may be because no one knows who he really is. And Charlie Manson is still famous and he
just killed a starlet and some hairdressers. But who
knows if he'll stand the test of time. I mean, you can
easily kill someone and just be overlooked—unless
you kill a lot of people, or kill a few people but in a
really ghastly way—but it would have to be so
ghastly.

Ms. Asquith: You . . . you've given this a lot of
thought.

Miss Riverton: I have. I mean, if there was another way—but I *can't* write a novel, I *can't* become a movie star, I can't invent a vaccine—because I have no talent. Not that talent is any guarantee of fame, but with talent I'd have had a shot at it, an honest shot. And I'd have taken it. I didn't want an easy way out. I didn't *want* to resort to murder. But fame is fame. The important thing to me is not to . . . just pass through. To leave a mark. To change the world. To have people's consciousness enlarged to include me. And it wasn't for material gain, I didn't want to get rich. I wasn't going to live well from my crime. If I got caught I'd probably be electrocuted. So, in a way, I would have been sacrificing my life for immortality—just like an artist or a scientist does. I would have been driven to kill not for the reward, but because there was nothing else I could do to fulfill myself—the same reason an artist creates. My curse has always been that I'm a special person with no special ability.

Ms. Asquith: Yes. That . . . is a problem.

Miss Riverton: And then, as the years passed, I realized how hard it is to meet someone famous and I thought maybe if I just killed someone rich and important or socially prominent. But by then I knew I was compromising. I was just after fame, not lasting fame. I told myself some fame is better than no fame—(*Shrugs, sighs*)—and I was probably right.

Ms. Asquith: Well . . . not . . . not necessarily. Lasting fame is . . . is by far . . . but why all this talk about fame. There's . . . there's so much more. To life. Than fame. There's . . . self-esteem, how well you've done with what you've had . . . love. Love is important.

Miss Riverton: That's just what Oprah said.

Ms. Asquith: Did she? Well, she's a very wise woman in many ways.

Miss Riverton: She's very famous.

Ms. Asquith: Yes, indeed.

Miss Riverton: She'd be a good one to kill.

Ms. Asquith: Excellent. Yes. You'd want someone that famous.

Miss Riverton: Sometimes that backfires.

Ms. Asquith: Hardly ever.

Miss Riverton: Oh, yes. The celebrity of the victim is so great it overshadows the assassin. That was the real triumph of Charles Manson. He killed people who were just rich and famous enough. That, of course, was what I didn't realize when I was a kid. I aimed too high.

Ms. Asquith: You know, Joan—may I call you Joan?

Miss Riverton: Of course, Miss Asquith.

Ms. Asquith: Margaret. Please. You know, Joan, things don't always work out as happily as they did for Charlie Manson. Sometimes there's a terrible murder and it's fun for a while—and then people forget—or there's another, *worse* murder and they're distracted. And, meanwhile, the poor murderer is imprisoned or electrocuted with no real reward for his crime. What was so important to him—or her—has been forgotten by everyone else. How far away is this restaurant you ordered from? Tokyo? Just joking. But it has been a long time since you ordered.

Miss Riverton: I've made you nervous, haven't I?

Ms. Asquith: What? Not at all.

Miss Riverton: Yes, I have. I've ruined everything. We were having such a nice time, one of the nicest times I've ever had and I ruined it.

Ms. Asquith: Nonsense. You've ruined nothing. Talking about murder is . . . just a little . . . always a little . . . edgy . . . but it's been such a long day . . . and I'm sure we're both . . . Would you like some music? Why don't I put on some music. (*She rises*) That's interesting. I can't move my legs. I have no feeling from the waist down. Something very strange is happening to me . . .

Miss Riverton: Miss Asquith . . .

Ms. Asquith: . . . It's as though somebody has put something in my food or my drink . . .

Miss Riverton: Miss Asquith! You've had half a bottle of wine on an empty stomach. And I've had the other half. We're both going to feel strange.

Ms. Asquith: Oh, yes. I forgot about the wine. How quickly the brain cells die. Now let's see—the music—

(*She staggers over to the remote, presses it, and* A Night On Bald Mountain *blares out*)

Ms. Asquith: Wrong music.

(*She presses the button again.* Death and Transfiguration *comes on, then a Philip Glass piece*)

Ms. Asquith: Don't I have one fucking song in this whole stupid collection?

Miss Riverton: You asked me to get classical. You said it would serve the clients better.

Ms. Asquith: Oh, of course. I was just talking to myself.

Miss Riverton: Oh, Miss Asquith, I think I should go. I've really upset you. Your hands are shaking.

Ms. Asquith: Well, I haven't eaten and it's late . . . so you might want to go . . . because it's late. But you certainly shouldn't go because you think you've upset me.

Miss Riverton: You know, this was just a hypothetical discussion. It's not like I would really kill someone. I'm not like some madman who gets fired from the post office and shoots everyone for revenge. I have no reason to do anything bad to anyone.

Ms. Asquith: That's right. And you never will.

Miss Riverton: I'm just this little secretary who makes $30,000 a year and that's all I'll ever be. Because that's all I'm worth. I've accepted that.

Ms. Asquith: No! Joan! What are you talking about. You're worth . . . everything.

Miss Riverton: But you're only paying me $30,000 and I don't think you'd pay me less than I'm worth.

Ms. Asquith: I . . . I . . . would . . . pay you more . . . if I could . . .

Miss Riverton: But why should you? I make so many mistakes . . .

Ms. Asquith: Well, now, Joan, that's true, isn't it? A little true. You do make mistakes. So I tell you what—when you stop making so *many* mistakes—I will give you a very nice raise.

Miss Riverton: Oh, Miss Asquith . . . I'm going to do you think . . . maybe some day I can become an assistant?

Ms. Asquith: Yes! Well! How about today?

Miss Riverton: Do you mean it?

Ms. Asquith: Absolutely. I'm not going to pay a mere secretary more than $30,000 a year—and that's what you'll be getting when I give you your raise— more than $30,000 a year.

Miss Riverton: How much more?

Ms. Asquith: We'll see.

Miss Riverton: Some secretaries make a hundred thousand a year.

Ms. Asquith: Very, very few.

Miss Riverton: I . . . I wish I could be sure you're not doing this because . . . in some way . . . I made you nervous. I would feel so awful if you were just being nice to me as . . . a kind of . . . out of fear.

Ms. Asquith: Don't be ridiculous. Do I seem to you to be the kind of person who would be intimidated into giving an employee a raise? And why would you make me nervous? Because when you were younger you wanted to kill someone famous? Hey! Who hasn't wanted to . . . pick up a gun and shoot a few famous people . . . at one time or another . . .

Miss Riverton: Actually, I was only going to shoot a man. If it was a woman I was going to stab her or strangle her. Weaker victim, lighter weapon.

Ms. Asquith: So many rules. And so fair.

Miss Riverton: Oh, yes. Of course, it's risky to be fair. If you try to stab or strangle a woman and her strength is too close to yours she can inflict so much injury you won't get the knife in. That's one of the reasons I got so strong.

(*The phone rings. Ms. Asquith leaps up*)

Ms. Asquith: I'll get it. (*Snatching up the phone*) Hello? . . . Hi, Charles. How are you. *Where* are you? . . . Martha's Vineyard? What fun. Miss Riverton and I are just finishing the wine you wouldn't let me drink this afternoon. We're having dinner together. In the office. Just the two of us.

(*There is the sound of a buzzer*)

Miss Riverton: That'll be the food.

Ms. Asquith (*into phone*): And the delivery man is here and Miss Riverton is just going out to get our food now. She's walking out of the room . . . she's . . .

(*As Miss Riverton exits Ms. Asquith whips up the remote and turns the music on again, then speaks softly under it*)

Ms. Asquith: Charles! Miss Riverton is psychotic. She just told me she wants to kill someone famous— but now she just wants to kill someone important to *be* famous—she's just terrifying. No, no, no, I can't fire her. She's talking about the post office. I'd have to spend the rest of my life with a bodyguard. I want you to give her a raise. Give her a raise! She's playing some kind of Machiavellian game with me, some

kind of brilliant cat and mouse game, but I think I'm
safe if I just do whatever she says ...

(*She breaks off as Miss Riverton enters with the food*)

Ms. Asquith: I have to hang up now, Charles. Miss
Riverton is back and I don't want to keep her waiting.

(*Ms. Asquith hangs up and clicks off the stereo. Miss
Riverton begins unloading the food*)

Miss Riverton: We have everything! Everything we
could ever want.

Ms. Asquith: It smells very good.

Miss Riverton: This is so nice, isn't it? I mean, this
means so much to me. Well, I don't want to embar-
rass you.

Ms. Asquith (*studying her*): No.

Miss Riverton: Here's to a whole new ... what?

Ms. Asquith: You name it.

Miss Riverton: Oh, I'm so bad with words.

Ms. Asquith: I think you're pretty good.

Miss Riverton: Well, thank you. (*She looks up*)
You're looking at me ... so ... so hard.

Ms. Asquith: Well, you're in my line of vision.

Miss Riverton: Ballgame! Is that a good word?

Ms. Asquith: Excellent. That's an excellent word. And now that you're in my line of vision . . . I begin to see . . . how very clever you are.

Miss Riverton: Careful—or I'll ask for that raise now.

Ms. Asquith: How very, very clever. Miss Riverton, you're fascinating. This is fascinating. This is almost relaxing.

Miss Riverton: Is it?

Ms. Asquith: Oh, yes. Because there's nothing I can do, is there?

Miss Riverton: I think . . . I'm not following you too well.

Ms. Asquith: I mean once someone wants something more than life—they win. There's nothing you can threaten them with.

Miss Riverton: Like the Arabs who blow themselves up so they can go straight to paradise.

Ms. Asquith: Yes. See? You are following me, after all. We all have our version of paradise, Miss Riv-

erton. Yours is fame. And mine is to live. I'll do anything to live. So I lose.

Miss Riverton: Maybe you should eat something
before you drink the saki.

Ms. Asquith: I wonder if this is what Dostoyevsky
meant when he wrote about the voluptuousness of
surrender. Have you ever read Dostoyevsky's jour-
nals, Miss Riverton?

Miss Riverton: Who's Dostoyevsky? Stalin?

(*There is a stunned pause*)

Ms. Asquith: What?

Miss Riverton: Is Dostoyevsky Stalin?

Ms. Asquith: No. He's Dostoyevsky.

Miss Riverton: Oh. I just thought . . . you were talking about Hitler before. So I thought . . . maybe
Dostoyevsky is Stalin.

Ms. Asquith: Then who would Stalin be?

Miss Riverton: I don't know. I thought maybe that
was his real name—Stalin's. Like Tito was only a
nickname for . . . whoever Tito was. So I thought
maybe Stalin was a nickname for Dostoyevsky.

Ms. Asquith: No.

Miss Riverton: Well . . . I didn't know. I don't think that's such a big mistake—not knowing who Dostoyevsky is. I know who Stalin is—and he's the famous one.

Ms. Asquith: Miss Riverton, I don't think I can submit to you if you go on with this.

Miss Riverton: What do you mean?

Ms. Asquith: I mean, I can't play cat and mouse with a bimbo.

Miss Riverton: Please don't call me a bimbo, Miss Asquith. That really upsets me.

Ms. Asquith: Well, what else can I call you when you suddenly sound like every chauffeur I've ever been to bed with? It just makes me wonder if you're really as crazy as you pretend to be. Or as strong.

Miss Riverton: I don't know what you're talking about.

Ms. Asquith: I'm talking about your strength, Miss Riverton, this strength with which you're going to strangle or stab a woman. And I'm wondering if the idea of presenting yourself as strong didn't come from my saying that the appearance of strength is power. And then . . . just building from there . . .

Miss Riverton: I'm not presenting myself as anything. (*Rising*) I'm not a bimbo. And I'm very strong.

Ms. Asquith: As strong as I am?

Miss Riverton: As strong as you are? (*She laughs*) Oh, I think so!

Ms. Asquith: But you also think Dostoyevsky is Stalin so your opinions aren't as informed as they might be.

Miss Riverton: You saw me carry the file boxes.

Ms. Asquith: No, I didn't.

Miss Riverton: You said you did.

Ms. Asquith: I lied.

Miss Riverton: Well . . . I carried them.

Ms. Asquith: Really? So did I.

Miss Riverton: You carried file boxes?

Ms. Asquith: Yes.

Miss Riverton: How many?

Ms. Asquith: How many did you carry?

Miss Riverton: When?

Ms. Asquith: Any time. The time you carried the most.

Miss Riverton: Six.

Ms. Asquith: So did I.

Miss Riverton: You carried six file boxes?

Ms. Asquith: Absolutely.

(*Miss Riverton studies her for several moments . . . then drops to the floor*)

Miss Riverton: Can you do this?

(*She does several marine push-ups*)

Ms. Asquith: Yes.

Miss Riverton: Let's see.

Ms. Asquith: Take my word for it.

Miss Riverton: You can't, can you? I'll bet you don't have the strength to do even one.

Ms. Asquith: Sheer physical strength isn't that necessary, Miss Riverton. Will counts, too.

Miss Riverton: No, it doesn't. Because a strong person can make a weak person do something *against* his will. He can destroy a weak person's will by using physical force. And then the weak person is always in his power.

Ms. Asquith: Isn't that just a wee bit dramatic for what is, essentially, a push-up contest?

Miss Riverton: Get down on the ground and try a push-up, Miss Asquith. I challenge you.

Ms. Asquith: I don't accept challenges. It would mean I have something to prove.

Miss Riverton: You'll accept this one. It's time for us to measure. (*Taking a step toward her*) I'm afraid I have to insist. (*She takes another step*)

Ms. Asquith (*quickly*): Well, if it's that important to you . . .

(*Miss Asquith gets slowly down, brushes away some dust on the rug, sits back up*)

Miss Riverton: See? You can't do it. But don't give up trying. Keep using that will of yours. You see? (*She picks up the exercise rubber*) This is trash. I put it right where it belongs. In the trash basket. It doesn't do anything. It doesn't make you strong. It's just a toy that gives you the illusion of strength—a personal trainer's silly invention for silly rich women. You know what makes you strong? Carrying file boxes, climbing three flights of stairs to a walk-up so you can afford to live in Manhattan, lugging groceries, walking miles to save money on subways, doing your own housework, wheeling your mother around when you visit her because you can't afford a nurse, painting your own ceiling, fixing your own pipes because the plumber costs so much. Hard, terrible labor—that's what makes you strong. And it's insane to think that God would create a world so lopsided that a multi-millionaire who hires a trainer to get her little hour of physical labor would be as strong as someone who actually . . .

(*She breaks off as Ms. Asquith suddenly rises up in a marine push-up . . . and then another . . . and then another . . . and then another*)

Ms. Asquith: You're right! It's not will. But it *is* that personal trainer. And I've been skipping sessions. (*Exultantly*) Well, it would be very hard to get that knife in me, Miss Riverton, would it inflict a lot of damage—if you were looking for a victim I mean. You'd have to stab me in the back and break your rules—and I know you wouldn't do that. You see, Jane, I'm afraid God *did* create a lopsided world. In that way he's very much like Tito. (*Miss Riverton turns away*) Well, now don't cry. That's no way to end a contest. Don't cry. It's not so bad. Although that walk-up doesn't sound wonderful. But look at those leg muscles. Oh, that food smells so good. (*She sits down and pats the sofa; Miss Riverton rises, obediently, and sits down beside her*) Think of it this way. Everything's just the same as it was this morning. And you weren't crying then. Now let's have our picnic, shall we? It's getting late. And get my exercise elastic out of the trash.

Miss Riverton: You're not going to fire me?

Ms. Asquith: Never. You're going to be the reason I
  stay in shape.

Virtual
Reality

by
Alan Arkin

A man comes into a room. It is dark. We don't see him clearly. From the other side of the room there is a cough. The man who has just entered, whose name is Lefty, speaks.

Lefty: Hello?

De Recha: Who's there?

Lefty: It's me. Lefty.

De Recha: Identify yourself.

Lefty: What?

De Recha: Identify yourself.

Lefty: I just did.

De Recha: No you didn't.

Lefty: I don't know what you mean.

De Recha: What do I need, a thesaurus? You know what identify yourself means. How do I know it's you?

Lefty: How does anyone know who's anybody?

De Recha: Look, we don't have time for oriental philosophy right now. We're in a sensitive situation here. All I'm asking for is a simple ID.

Lefty: I left my wallet at home.

De Recha: You left your wallet at home.

Lefty: That's right.

De Recha: That was smart wasn't it?

Lefty: No one said anything about bringing ID.

De Recha: You wander around the streets with no ID?

Lefty: Sometimes.

De Recha: What would you do if a cop stopped you?

Lefty: I don't know.

De Recha: How would anyone know where to take you if you were in an accident?

Lefty: They'd take me to a hospital like they take anyone. What is this bullshit?

De Recha: What about the insurance?

Lefty: What about what insurance?

De Recha: Medical insurance.

Lefty: What's this got to do with anything? I have no ID. Okay?

De Recha: So give me something else.

Lefty: Like what? If I have no ID, what can I give you? What other kind of thing do I have that you could want?

De Recha: What have you got?

Lefty: What do you want to see? You want to see a fingerprint? A hair sample? You want to look at my shoe? What do you want to see?

De Recha: Listen—what the hell did you come here thinking? We're in a sensitive situation. You don't know me, I don't know you, there's got to be some kind of way of identifying you. Otherwise you could be anyone.

Lefty: You want to hear about my past? Specific little things from my youth? What do you want?

De Recha: No, I would have no way to corroborate them.

Lefty: Why not?

De Recha: I'd need extensive files. Things to refer to. I don't have shit here. All I have is a couple of items in my head that they gave me.

Lefty: Like what?

De Recha: I can't tell you.

Lefty: Who the hell asked you to tell me? Use them to *question* me. You said you have items in your head. What good are they if you don't use them?

De Recha: They don't pertain to the question of the ID.

Lefty: Then what *do* they pertain to?

De Recha: They pertain to things we're supposed to discuss once the ID has been ascertained.

(*There is an uncomfortable pause*)

Lefty: So what do you want me to do?

De Recha: Give me a minute. I gotta think this through. (*He thinks for a minute*) Come over here.

Lefty (*suspiciously*): What for?

De Recha: So's I can get a look at you.

Lefty: Then what will you know?

De Recha: I'll know *that*.

(*Lefty sighs and walks over to De Recha out of the gloom. They look at each other for a long time. Nothing seems to have been resolved*)

Lefty: So?

(There is a pause. De Recha seems to be thinking, but we don't really know)

Lefty (*continuing*): *So?*

De Recha: I'm lost.

Lefty: You want me to come in again?

De Recha: No.

Lefty: It might clear your head.

De Recha: Shut up a minute. I'm trying to sort this out.

Lefty: I'm coming in again. (*He starts to go out*)

De Recha (*in an attempt to stop him*): Wait. Wait.

(Lefty comes in again. They stand. Lefty seems to be getting slightly impatient)

Lefty: Now ask me.

De Recha: Ask you what?

Lefty: Ask me to identify myself for Christ's sake.

De Recha: Why? We'll be in the same boat as before.

Lefty: I'll try something different.

De Recha: But I will still do the same thing. So where will we be then? (*Lefty pauses himself for a long time, staring at De Recha, then starts to leave*) What's this now? Where you going?

Lefty: There's confusion here. There's disarray. It makes me uncomfortable. I like to work in an atmosphere of mutual respect and camaraderie.

De Recha: Don't run off on me. Don't take it personal. I can't have you on this job without knowing who you are. I have to be sure. You'd do the same thing in my place. Come on don't be like that.

Lefty: Well, I have to be sure too. This is not my normal operational context. I'm not used to working with people I don't know either.

De Recha: Please. Don't start showing off now. Don't use this slight awkwardness as an opportunity to throw fancy words at me. That's a power ploy. I don't like that.

Lefty: I'm getting really, really pissed off.

De Recha: What for? What did I do?

Lefty: You're confusing me. I don't like confusion. I don't like mental disorders of any kind. I don't like disarray.

De Recha: Are you accusing me of mental disorder?

Lefty: No, no. Mental *disorders*. Disorders. I don't like chaos.

De Recha: I'm only doing what they told me to do. You work for them too. I take orders from them, you take orders from me, that's the way it works.

Lefty: Well, they picked the wrong guy to give orders.

De Recha: They picked me, so maybe they picked the right guy. What are you, upset because they didn't pick you?

Lefty: Don't psychoanalyze me. Now or ever. I'm not getting into my inner workings with you. I came here to do a job. No one told me about any fucking ID's, no one told me about wallets, they told me to show up.

De Recha: And what they told *me* is about asking you to identify yourself. We're in the same boat.

Lefty: But I *did* identify myself.

De Recha: No you didn't.

Lefty: Yes I did.

De Recha: No you didn't, and please try not to get upset. I asked you for identification and you couldn't give me any. Do you remember that?

Lefty: You asked me who I was. Do you remember that?

De Recha: Yes I do.

Lefty: So who did I say I was?

De Recha: You said you were Lefty.

Lefty: So?

De Recha: So what?

Lefty: So what do you think identifying yourself means? And what the fuck do you think I did? You asked me who I was, I told you. Right?

De Recha: Right.

Lefty: Who were you expecting?

De Recha: Lefty.

Lefty: So, you asked me, I told you, that's that. We're straight, we're organized, we know who we are.

De Recha: Okay. Okay. When you're right you're right. Well, maybe things got a little bit out of hand.

Lefty: Don't worry about it.

De Recha: You see, I'm new in this particular job; I've never done anything like this before and I want to do it right. Identify means ID to me. I wish they'd have told me a simple giving of a name would be enough. But there's no harm done. We're straight now. (*He waits for some corroboration from Lefty, a look, something . . . nothing comes*) Anyhow. Let's get on with it.

Lefty: Fine by me.

De Recha: Let's go over the job.

Lefty: Let's do it.

(*They both take off their jackets, look for places to hang them, find none, both put jackets back on*)

De Recha: Okay. We start. First thing—the equipment comes.

Lefty: Check.

De Recha: We examine it carefully, making sure all parts are as specified.

Lefty: Check.

De Recha: To do that, we check it against the way bill.

Lefty: Check. Where's the way bill?

De Recha: It's with the equipment.

Lefty (*looking around*): And where's the equipment?

De Recha: It's on its way.

Lefty: On its way where?

De Recha: It's on its way here.

Lefty: When?

De Recha: Right now.

Lefty: Well, that's good, because if the schedule is going to be adhered to, we don't have a hell of a lot of time.

De Recha: It's going to be close. Don't think I'm not aware of that fact. (*Lefty checks his watch. They sit. They scratch. They surreptitiously scrutinize each other*) Okay. While we're waiting, let's go over the equipment.

Lefty: The equipment isn't here.

De Recha: I know what it *is*.

Lefty: But *I* don't know what it is.

De Recha: So I'll tell you what it is.

(*Lefty is beginning to get tense. A peculiar dislocation begins to appear in his eyes*)

De Recha (*continuing*): First thing. The equipment gets delivered right over here. There will be three boxes. Inside the first box will be the way bill, the

manual for the materials and our specific instructions, among other things. So that's it. Let's do a dry
run.

Lefty: Of what?

De Recha: Of assembly. Let's see how long it will
take us.

Lefty: To do what?

De Recha: To get everything organized and put together.

Lefty: We don't have anything here.

De Recha: We'll do a mock up.

Lefty: We can't do that.

De Recha: Yes we can.

Lefty: No we can't. A mock up is when you have a
dummy of the real thing. We don't have a dummy of
the real thing. We don't have anything.

De Recha: We will in a minute.

Lefty: So we'll do it then. When it comes.

De Recha: No, there won't be time.

Lefty: So you want us to do a check right now of
imaginary things but when the real things get here

we're not going to bother? We just go with the flow? Is that what I'm hearing?

De Recha: I want to do a dry run. Do you have a problem with that? Did I get the terminology okay? Did you like my wording?

Lefty: I'm not going to do this.

De Recha (*holding on to himself, and the beginnings of his own frustrations*): Look, I gotta tell you, I'm getting a little tired of being stonewalled. You're bucking me on every turn. I keep getting this resistance. Are you aware of that? Is that something you do on purpose or is it an unconscious thing with you?

Lefty: I'm not stonewalling anybody. I just want to do what I was hired to do. I don't want to do pantomimes.

De Recha: The problem with you is insubordination. I don't think you like me. You want to be boss or something. I gotta remind you that I take orders from you know who, and you take orders from me. That's the way it works. What's the deal? Is that so hard to understand?

Lefty: I don't take orders from anyone. I was hired to do a specific job, for which I am highly qualified, and then I do what I do. In my own way. You supply the equipment, you give me the time of occurrence and any particulars that you might need, and the rest is up to me.

De Recha: Why don't you take orders from people?

Lefty: I just don't take orders from people. I work for myself. I'm a lone wolf. That's what I am, that's what I do.

De Recha: What's the big deal about taking orders from people?

Lefty: I don't like it. I don't do it and I don't like it. End of report.

De Recha: Everybody takes orders from somebody. That's the way it works.

Lefty: That's not the way I work. I'm not talking about this.

De Recha: That's the way the whole world works. What, are you some kind of outcast from society? You can't work within a structure?

Lefty: Right.

De Recha: You'll never amount to anything. You'll be doomed to a life of loneliness. The whole world calls out to accept, to join in, to be part of a larger thing, and you're going the other way.

Lefty (*losing his patience completely*): Okay, let's go. Let's do the pantomime. Where's the fucking box?

De Recha: I don't know if it's a good idea now.

Lefty: Come on, stop the guilt making. Let's open the fucking boxes.

De Recha: What's the sudden shift in attitude? Are you interested in opening the boxes now because you want to or because I told you to?

Lefty: What difference does it make. Let's open the boxes. Where are they? Where are the boxes? (*He looks around for the imaginary boxes*) Come on let's go. Let's do it. Let's go.

De Recha: You didn't answer my question.

Lefty: I said what difference does it make?

De Recha: It makes a difference my friend because attitude is everything. The way you approach work is the way the work turns out. You have a negative attitude, it affects everyone and everything around you.

Lefty: Screw you.

De Recha: Yeah, right. Screw me. Very good. (*He laughs*) This from a guy who will have my life in his hands in about an hour. Screw me. Is that supposed to have me brimming over with feelings of confidence? And you wonder why I'm concerned about your attitude?

Lefty: I don't give a shit what you wonder about. Come on, let's open the fucking boxes.

De Recha: I've lost my incentive. I don't really feel like doing it now.

Lefty: Let's open the fucking boxes!

De Recha: Okay but remember this is your idea now. I've lost my zest for it.

Lefty: Let's just open the fucking boxes.

De Recha: Okay we'll open the boxes.

Lefty (*eager to get on with it*): Where are they?

De Recha: Right here.

Lefty: Okay. Good. Let's get started. Where's box number one? (*He looks around*)

De Recha: Right there.

Lefty: Okay, so here it is. Here's box number one. (*He points somewhere in the air*) Let's dive in, we'll get the bill of lading and we're off. (*He starts opening a box*)

De Recha: You gotta pry it open.

Lefty: So then it's not a box. It's a crate.

De Recha: It's more than likely a crate.

Lefty: So we're opening a box, a crate, what?

De Recha: Let's say it's a crate.

Lefty: Okay, we're saying it's a crate. And we pry open the crate with what?

De Recha: They'll more than likely leave us a crowbar.

Lefty: They'll more than likely leave us a crowbar. (*And he addresses an imaginary assistant*) Okay hand me that crowbar, Joe, thanks a lot, Joe, now I'm prying open the crate. (*Lefty starts prying open a good-sized crate. He's not too good at the pantomime, but he's trying to behave himself*) Okay, the crate is open. And here's the bill of lading. Okay, okay everything looks good.

De Recha: I gotta look at it.

Lefty: Okay, pardon me, here you go, give the way bill a little look. (*De Recha takes the paper from Lefty, looks at it forever. Lefty waits and waits and then—*) This is bullshit. I gotta get out of here.

(*He starts to head for the door again*)

De Recha (*irate*): Now what's wrong?

Lefty: What's wrong? I wouldn't know where to begin.

De Recha: What set you off this time?

Lefty: I don't want to talk about it.

De Recha: I think we should talk about it.

Lefty: I don't want to talk about it.

De Recha: You have to talk about it.

Lefty: I don't have to talk about shit.

De Recha: Is that what I tell the boys upstairs? They ask me, "What happened?" I say, "He took off." "Why?" they ask. I say, "He took offense at the way I looked at the way bill." What do you think they're going to go through when I tell them that?

Lefty: Is that a threat?

De Recha: It's a fact of life and it's a question.

Lefty: It's a threatening question.

De Recha: It's a legitimate question. You run off; I'm left holding the bag. What do you want me to do, lie? You want me to take a fall for you? I don't even know you.

Lefty: You took a half an hour reading the fucking way bill.

De Recha: So?

Lefty: So there's nothing there. You're standing there reading thin air. That's what ticked me off. Think about it for a minute. Think about what that looks like. There's nothing in there. I'm standing here like some moron, watching you reading your fuck-

ing fist. You're holding up nothing and you're reading your fucking fist.

De Recha: I'm reading the way bill.

Lefty: So read it faster.

De Recha: There's got to be about fifty items on
there.

Lefty: When it *gets* here.

De Recha: That's right.

Lefty: So when the real list gets here, read that one
slow. This one read fast.

De Recha: There won't be time.

Lefty: Okay read it any way you want. What do I
care? (*He paces*) Listen, let me tell you something.
I'm beginning to feel manipulated. I'm beginning to
think you're not as dumb as you're pretending to
be, that there's some insidious purpose behind all
of this bullshit. That's what I think. You're freaking
me out. And on top of that, I think you're doing it on
purpose.

De Recha: I don't do anything on purpose.

Lefty: Whatever that means. Go ahead and read the
way bill.

Left to Right: Jeannie Berlin, Elaine May in *The Way of all Fish*, one of the comedies in **Power Plays**.

*All photos of the Off Broadway production of **Power Plays** by Chris Bennion.*

Anthony Arkin (left) and Alan Arkin in *Virtual Reality*.

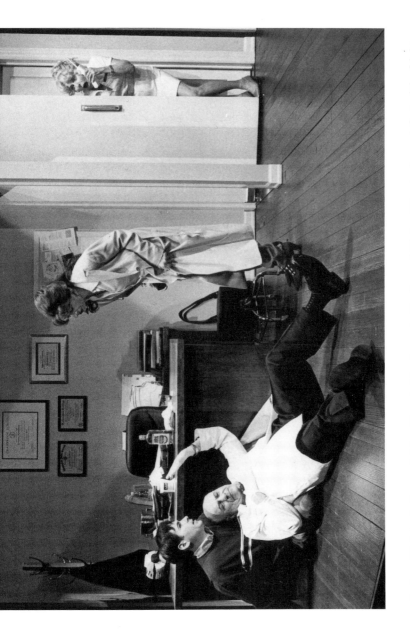

Left to Right: Anthony Arkin, Alan Arkin, Jeannie Berlin and Elaine May in *In and Out of the Light*.

Elaine May and Alan Arkin.

De Recha: What will you be doing while I'm reading the way bill?

Lefty: What will I be doing? Say! I have an idea! Why don't I open up the other crates!

De Recha: Good thinking. Have you got a pencil?

Lefty: Yes.

(He hands De Recha a real pencil. De Recha makes notes with the real pencil on the imaginary way bill. The crate tops have been opened. With each crate the miming gets a bit better)

Lefty *(continuing)*: The crates are open.

De Recha: All of them?

Lefty: Every last one.

De Recha: They're completely open?

Lefty: They couldn't be more open if they tried.

De Recha: Alright then.

Lefty: You ready?

De Recha: I'm ready.

Lefty: Okay start calling off the items, I'll find them, you check them off.

De Recha: The other way around. You find an item, you call it out, I check it off.

Lefty: I can't do that.

De Recha: Why not?

Lefty: Because I don't know what's in the crates. That's why not.

De Recha (*he sighs*): Just look in the fucking crates, pull an item out, name the item, I check it off the list, on to the next. What's so hard about that?

Lefty: What's the address here?

De Recha: 243 and a half Hope Street, why?

(*Lefty pulls out a piece of paper from his pocket and studies it carefully. He puts the paper back in his pocket*)

De Recha (*continuing*): Everything okay?

Lefty (*trying to be intimate and warm*): Look. Let me be honest with you. I'm lost. I can't work this way. I'm used to a certain pattern. I've been doing things one way for a long time, and for better or for worse, it works for me that way. This is . . . this is . . . well, I don't know what this is. This is something different. And it's probably great, it's probably some new and innovative . . . thing . . . but I'm kind of an old fashioned guy and I just can't get with this. It's too convoluted.

De Recha: Which means . . . ?

Lefty: Which means—and I hate doing this to you, being that it's such short notice and everything— but I've got to get out of here. I have to give notice. No hard feelings, I go my way you go yours, and we forget about the whole thing.

De Recha: Wait a minute now. This is very bad news you're giving me.

Lefty: Well, I can't help it. It can't be helped.

De Recha: Can't be helped? You're leaving me a sitting duck with no support system. I'm in a deep hole because of you. I'm completely unnerved now.

Lefty: I hate doing it to you.

De Recha: Also, you've been given a very generous advance. What happens with that?

Lefty: I'll get it back to you.

De Recha: That's not the issue. You were given the advance to secure your services. To guarantee them. We start moving in ninety minutes. Who am I going to find to replace you in ninety minutes?

Lefty: Look, you're calling on my honor as a professional, and that's a serious issue. But I'm telling you, the way things are going I'm not going to be able to function with any degree of precision. You want that? You want me frustrated and confused?

De Recha: I just want you to comply with what's being asked of you, which is to be flexible for a few minutes in a test situation.

Lefty: It's an unorthodox test situation.

De Recha: Does that make it wrong?

Lefty: It makes it uncomfortable.

De Recha: That's why we're doing the test. To make it comfortable. Is that such a big deal?

Lefty: No.

De Recha: Okay then. You want to find me an item?

Lefty: All right then.

De Recha: All right then.

(*Grudgingly, Lefty starts digging into a box. He pulls something out and looks at it for a while*)

De Recha (*continuing*): Well?

(*Lefty continues to look at the item in his hand*)

De Recha (*continuing*): What's the problem?

Lefty: I can't tell what this is.

De Recha: Oh for Christ's sake.

(*De Recha walks over and pulls the thing out of Lefty's hand. He looks it over, then throws it back at Lefty disgustedly, and checks off something on the way bill*)

Lefty: What is it?

De Recha: An inflatable air mattress. You ever seen an inflatable air mattress before?

Lefty: Yeah.

De Recha: So why do you have trouble identifying an inflatable air mattress? Do you have a problem with indecisiveness? Well, this is a hell of a time for me to find out, isn't it? (*No answer*) Isn't it?

Lefty: Yes. But I have to say that an inflatable air mattress is not something I would have expected on this assignment.

De Recha: Well, when *you* pick the equipment, you leave out the inflatable air mattress. When *we* pick the equipment, we put in whatever we goddamn well please. Once again I have to remind you that my life is going to be in your hands in about an hour. Now do you want to go and meditate on that in a corner somewhere, or can we continue what is really a very simple procedure?

Lefty: Sorry.

De Recha: That's all right. Give me the next item.

Lefty (*holding up the air mattress*): Where do I put this? (*No answer*) Is there any particular place you'd like me to put it? (*No answer*) I'll just sit it down over here, then.

(*Lefty puts the air mattress down, somewhere away from the crate. He goes back to the crate and digs out the next item. He looks it over*)

De Recha: And? Well?

Lefty: It's confusing.

De Recha: In what sense?

Lefty: It's got a lot of different attributes.

De Recha: So describe the attributes.

Lefty: Well, it's fairly light weight, and I can't tell what material it's made out of.

De Recha: Is it soft or hard?

Lefty: It's kind of in between.

De Recha: You want to give me some fucking definition? So I can find something vaguely corresponding on the way bill? You want to give me a little hint?

Lefty: Okay, okay. I think it's plastic. It's . . . it . . . it seems to be plastic.

De Recha: It *seems* to be plastic.

Lefty: Yes. It seems to be plastic.

De Recha: Seems to be . . . ? You want to go completely crazy and say it's plastic?

Lefty: Let's call it plastic. (*No response. Waits*) It's plastic. It's definitely plastic.

De Recha (*with enormous sarcasm*): Good boy! Way to go! Okay! We got plastic! Does it open up? Has it got a thing on it that opens?

Lefty: I . . . I . . . (*He's freezing up a bit*) I can't tell.

(*De Recha goes over to Lefty, takes the item out of Lefty's hand, opens and closes a latch and then sets it down. He goes back to his place and checks it off on the way bill*)

Lefty (*continuing*): What was it?

De Recha: A first-aid kit.

Lefty: Right. Right. That was my hunch. I had a feeling that's what it was, it kind of felt like a first-aid kit, but it wasn't like the kinds of first-aid kits I've seen before.

De Recha: It was a plain first-aid kit, like you get in a drug store. Like you get in a hardware store. Like you get in an automotive supply store.

Lefty: Well I don't spend a lot of time in any of those places.

De Recha: Oh, I see.

(*De Recha goes over to where he put down the kit, picks it up and puts it under Lefty's nose*)

Lefty: What?

De Recha: What does that say?

Lefty (*he tries to read*): It says . . . first-aid kit.

(*De Recha throws the kit back on the floor*)

De Recha: Next.

(*Lefty digs into the box. He pulls out an item. Holds it up*)

Lefty: What's this? An alarm clock.

(*De Recha shakes his head no*)

Lefty (*continuing*): A timer of some kind? With wires coming out of the back.

De Recha: Oh yeah, timer, I got it.

Lefty: A timing device. (*He looks at it suspiciously*) What are we doing with a timing device? What do we need that for?

De Recha: We'll discuss the action after we make sure of the material.

Lefty: A timing device. That's a little out of left field, to me.

De Recha: Next.

Lefty: Books.

De Recha: What kind of books?

Lefty: A Sanskrit/English dictionary.

De Recha: Check.

Lefty: *Walden.* By Henry David Thoreau.

De Recha: Check.

Lefty: Nice edition.

De Recha: Next.

Lefty: It starts to make an odd kind of pattern, doesn't it?

De Recha: Not to me.

Lefty: Well, to me it starts to suggest things.

De Recha: Like what?

Lefty: That's not clear yet. It's hanging right below the surface.

De Recha: Next patient.

Lefty: Looks like fruits and nuts. Dried fruits and nuts.

De Recha: Check.

Lefty: Interesting. Here's another one.

De Recha: Another what?

Lefty: Another box of fruits and nuts.

De Recha: Can't be.

Lefty: Why not?

De Recha: The way bill says there's only one box of fruits and nuts.

Lefty: Well, here's another one.

De Recha: Oh, God. This isn't good. I don't like this. It's an inconsistency. I don't like inconsistencies.

Lefty: So what do we do with it?

De Recha (*he thinks for a minute*): It's extra, let's open the bastard up.

(*De Recha opens it up and looks inside. Taking a handful*)

De Recha (*continuing*): Mmm. Apricots and almonds. Nice combo. Help yourself.

Lefty: I'm not hungry.

De Recha: Put some in your pocket for later. You never know when you'll need a little something.

(*De Recha digs into the box, puts a big handful into Lefty's jacket pocket*)

De Recha (*continuing*): Next item.

Lefty: Rollerskates. Two pairs of rollerskates.

De Recha: Check.

Lefty (*he loses it*): Jesus Christ, what is all this? This is a miscellaneous bunch of shit here. What are we doing? Are we doing a job? Are we doing a serious piece of work or are we putting on some vaudeville show? What's going on? It's like some circus bull-shit.

De Recha: Next.

Lefty: What are we doing with rollerskates?

De Recha: Next.

Lefty: Are you expecting me to use rollerskates?

De Recha: Next.

Lefty: I don't know how.

De Recha: Next.

Lefty: For the record, I don't do rollerskating. Just put that down. Put it on a margin of the fucking way bill. Put down I don't know how to rollerskate.

De Recha: It will be duly noted. Boy, you're a sensitive fellow, aren't you? Kind of a nervous Nancy? Is that what they sent me? A nervous Nancy kind of guy?

Lefty: No, no. But this starts to add up to something, doesn't it? I mean it's not just a random mishmash they threw together.

De Recha: Next.

Lefty: I mean we have a specific function, let's face it. We have a job to do. These things are supposed to be for that job, aren't they?

De Recha: Next!

Lefty (*he's getting no satisfaction*): Christ. (*He goes back to the crate. Continuing*) Two hurricane lanterns.

(*He sets them in the pile*)

De Recha: Check.

Lefty: But whatever this job is, it's not the job I signed up for. I hope you know that. What I do doesn't require rollerskates.

(Here Lefty paces, then walks back to where the lanterns are. He trips over the lanterns and we hear them clunk. It's the first sound we hear. He pulls something else out of the crate)

Lefty *(continuing)*: Two gas masks.

De Recha: Check.

Lefty: Gas masks? What do we need . . . Aw, forget it. Two thermal blankets.

De Recha: Check.

Lefty: What's this? *(He's fingering something small)* Passports. Two. Two Argentinian passports. *(He looks in one)*

De Recha: Check.

Lefty: This is me. That's my picture in here. *(He looks in the other)* And this is you. This is your picture. They've got my picture in a fake Argentine passport. Fuck this.

De Recha: Excuse me?

Lefty: I said fuck this. This has nothing to do with me, this isn't what I signed up for. This is a life situation you've got me in. This is a major operation. We've got gas masks, we've got Himalayan mountain gear, we've got timing devices, we've got passports. This isn't some little job, this is some kind of kamikaze life and death commitment thing. I can feel it.

De Recha: You don't feel anything.

Lefty: How do you know what I feel?

De Recha: Did you read the briefing material?

Lefty: No.

De Recha: Then shut up and finish unpacking the crate. How would you know what this adds up to? Since when are you a mission strategist?

Lefty: I can sense . . .

De Recha: You don't sense anything. Unpack the crate; we're running out of time here!

Lefty (*he grudgingly goes back to the crate*): A Max Factor make-up kit.

De Recha: What's in it?

(*Lefty sits with the box on his knees and opens it*)

Lefty: Two false noses, three pairs of eyeglasses, scar make-up, one mustache, two beards . . .

De Recha: Check.

Lefty: Why don't you give me some kind of hint? I'm being thrown into a life situation here, against my will, against my original deal and you don't even tell me what the rules are. Don't you think that's just the vaguest bit unfair? Look, I'm a stranger to you.

You've told me twice now that your life is going to be in my hands. Where's the trust that you're supposed to be placing in me? I have a right to know. How am I supposed to perform my work without some confidence being placed in me?

De Recha: Do you think I know what's happening? I'm in the same boat you are. The only difference between you and me is that I've learned to trust. That's why I'm steady as a rock here, and you're going into cardiac arrest. You tell me about this lone wolf shit with such pride . . . well here are the fruits of it. You can't trust. Whose hands are shaking? Not mine. Next.

(*Lefty grudgingly goes back to the crate*)

Lefty: Two bungie cords.

De Recha: Check.

Lefty: I'd really like to know why we need the fake noses and the beards. I wonder if it's some gag. If we're just being fucked with. This is locked.

(*De Recha throws him a key. Lefty fumbles with it*)

De Recha: I know what you're going through, Lefty, but believe me, there comes a time when you just have to let it all go. Jump into the void. That's how you grow. So what if there's a fake nose or two? What's the big deal? If it comes to it, if I'm told to put one on, I will. And with pride. And I'll trust that in the end the reason will be made clear to me, and I'll

be the better person for having worn it. If I needed
to know why now, someone would have told me.

(*Lefty gets the box open; a wind begins to come up*)

Lefty: Guns. Guns?

De Recha: Check.

Lefty: I thought there wasn't going to be any violence.

De Recha: Who told you that?

Lefty: It was in the deal that was set up originally. I
don't do violence. There wasn't going to be any violence.

De Recha: How can you guarantee a thing like that?

Lefty: How can you do it? You *guarantee* it. That's
how you do it. You say *there will be no violence*!

De Recha: We're not going to *instigate* any violence.
That I can tell you. But how do you guarantee something isn't going to happen? You walk down the
street, a car could lose its brakes, jump the curb and
kill you.

Lefty: Wait a minute. Wait a minute. This is
sophistry. This is bullshit. You don't need guns to
protect you from cars hitting you in the street. I
don't work with weapons. I've never fired a gun. I
have an aversion to them. My hands shake if I hold

a gun. I'm afraid of them. I'm deathly afraid of them. (*He goes grudgingly back to the crate*)

De Recha: It will be duly noted. What's the next item?

Lefty: A two-man tent.

De Recha: Instructions?

Lefty: Yes. Right here.

De Recha: Read them off.

(*Lefty rips the instructions off of the tent. De Recha through this speech picks up the crate and sets it down loudly on the far left side of the stage*)

Lefty: Look. I can't do the gun thing. It's that simple. I understand the thrill that danger presents, don't get me wrong. I understand it intellectually. Living life constantly in the moment of your death . . . it puts everything into excruciatingly sharp focus . . .

De Recha: Just read off the instructions.

Lefty (*reads from the sheet*): "The Asteroid Light is a free-standing tent and staking out the floor is not necessary. However, we recommend that it be staked after being pitched, for greater stability in high winds." Why did you pick me? You must have seen that my profile doesn't fit anything you're look-ing for.

De Recha: Read the instructions for Christ's sake. I'm going to lose my mind with your whining and moaning.

Lefty (*he reads*): "Unfurl the tent and lay the tent floor flat on the ground, with the door unzipped."

De Recha (*he does so, and very quickly. We hear it unzip and open*): Got it.

Lefty: "Unfold the shock-corded pole sections . . ."

De Recha: That's got to be these things . . . (*We hear them as he pulls them out of the bag*)

Lefty: ". . . and allow them to spring together. You will then have three poles of equal length."

De Recha: Here we go.

(*With Lefty's help they quickly put together the three poles. We hear the sounds*)

Lefty: That wasn't so bad.

De Recha: Let's go. We're losing the light.

Lefty: "Insert one pole into the pole sleeve, which runs from point A to point C. Insert another pole into the pole sleeve running from B to D. (*De Recha inserts poles. We hear the sounds*) Insert the metal tips of the pole ends into their respective grommets at points A and B, then from the opposite ends of the tent, push the poles into the pole sleeves, one at a time, make them flex into each other, until you can insert the metal tips of the poles in the grommets at points C and D. Next . . ."

De Recha: Whoa, slow down. I can't catch my breath. There's no oxygen up here.

Lefty: We should have come up slower.

De Recha: Then it would be dark by now.

Lefty: We have the lanterns.

De Recha: But no kerosene.

Lefty: "Drape the fly over the tent." You have to be a fucking engineer to understand the terminology here. How do you do this if you haven't done this before? My hands are freezing. I can't move my fingers.

De Recha: I'll put the fly up. You can just read.

Lefty: What's the fly? The flap? Is the flap the fly?

De Recha: It's got to be this; it's the only thing left. Just keep reading.

Lefty: My eyelids are frozen. I can't read the manual.

De Recha: Give me the fucking manual. (*He rips it out of Lefty's hand*) You're so busy duly noting things all the time, let me duly note you something:

This was a two man operation. It can't be done alone. We're doomed.

Lefty: No we're not. I'm here. I'm just cold is all. As soon as I warm up I'll go back to work.

De Recha: I don't want your help. You've done enough. You fixed me good. Yes you did, you bastard. And now I'm going to die out here.

Lefty: You're not going to die.

De Recha: I'm going to die out here because of you. I'm going to freeze to death. Away from friends and loved ones.

Lefty: Forgive me, I'm the one who's the injured party, if there is an injured party.

(*He is blowing on his fingers now and stamping to keep warm*)

Lefty (*continuing*): I came to do a job. And that's what I'm doing to the best of my ability.

De Recha: Some ability. You screwed everything up completely. You didn't even have the foresight to pull a couple of ski parkas out of that thing.

Lefty: I just followed the instructions. That's all I did.

De Recha: That's all you did? You were the crate man.

Lefty: I had nothing whatsoever to do with the crates.

De Recha: You named the stuff!

Lefty: I pulled things out. I didn't name anything.

De Recha: You defined the entire way bill.

Lefty: I defined nothing! I just called out what was there.

De Recha: Who made it there?

Lefty: Don't start that shit! Everything I called out you checked off. Every time I said "so and so," you said "check."

De Recha: Don't be so quick to decide my motives.

Lefty: Isn't that what happened?

De Recha: Yeah, but not for the reasons you think.

Lefty: What were the reasons?

De Recha: At each item I heard, my mind raced in horror.

Lefty: So why did you go on? Who told you to continue?

De Recha: I did it to calm you down. To appease you. To keep you from folding. To keep you from humil-

iating yourself with the boys upstairs. I did it to save
your ass.

(*He gets a thermal blanket from the pile, puts it on and
gets into the tent*)

De Recha (*continuing*): And now I'm paying for it. I
was a nice guy and now I'm going to die for my trouble.

Lefty: Let's stop the recriminations, okay, this is bullshit. And you're not going to die. We're in a precari-
ous situation and we need to pull together. We have
to go into survival mode. Where's the other blanket?

De Recha: How am I supposed to know? It's wherever you threw it. Am I supposed to do everything?

Lefty (*finds the other blanket, gets it on, gets into tent*):
Don't go to sleep. That's very dangerous at these
temperatures. Just stay awake. And no more argu-
ing.

De Recha: Everything I did was for your benefit. So
you would grow. So you would be up to this job,
now look what you've done. (*Sound of approaching
voices*) And now they're coming. Please God, let me
freeze to death before they get me. Please let me
die. Please don't let them get me.

Lefty: Before who gets you? What "who" are you talking about?

De Recha: Don't you hear them? They're coming.

Lefty: I can't hear anything. My ears are frozen. And nobody's coming.

De Recha: Yes they are. They're coming. And when they find us I think they are going to be very displeased.

Lefty: But why? What's happening? I don't understand anything. What went wrong? Everything was going so well. I felt myself growing. I felt that in spite of some initial confusion, I learned a great deal. I've learned patience and flexibility. I get along with people so much better. I'm a better person now, I swear it. Don't give up on me. Things are just getting good.

De Recha: No, it's over. I'm sick of your complaining. Of your whining, of your pretended incompetence, of your total unwillingness to comply with what's asked of you. Plus, and possibly worst of all, you're a fucking bore.

Lefty: You've had it in for me since the minute I walked in the warehouse, you bastard. Why? What did I do to you?

De Recha: You gave the impression that you had strengths and abilities past the ordinary man in the street. That you knew mysterious things.

Lefty: What the hell are you talking about? I didn't say anything about any of that. I showed up, that's all I did.

De Recha: It wasn't that. It wasn't what you did.

Lefty: What was it then?

De Recha: It was your *attitude*.

Lefty: My attitude?

De Recha: Yes.

Lefty: What bearing has my attitude on any of this?

De Recha: You gave the *impression*. The set of your head . . . little pauses . . . you allowed me to believe. You equivocated. You used inflection and gesture to your advantage.

Lefty: Forgive me, but I think you're raving now. None of this sounds familiar, and I think I can handle criticism at this point. I think it's the cold getting to you, or the altitude. I wouldn't make any judgements that you might be stuck with. Things are bad, they turned that way, but they can just as easily turn good. Wait and see.

De Recha: Shut up. I'm going to kill you now, and then myself.

Lefty: If you do, you'll be making a big mistake. You will live to regret it. This I can promise.

De Recha: Shut up. Before I kill you, I want you to know a few things. First of all, that none of this is personal, that I have no animosity whatsoever for you, and secondly, that it's for your own good. I can assure you that when it's over, you will be the better man for it.

(*Lefty has sunk to the ground during the preceding, and now he grabs a rock. He hurls the masks at De Recha. De Recha ducks and fires a deafening round, but he misses Lefty who then lunges at him. Lefty grabs the bungie cord and twists it around De Recha's neck. They fall to the floor in a violent struggle, ending up sitting with Lefty behind De Recha and strangling him*)

Lefty: How dare you tell me that it's not personal. Everything is personal. And nothing is for my own good, unless I am doing it. You can kill me. It makes no fucking difference to me at this point. But first I want you to know who I am. I want you to know something about this entity that you so blithely want to terminate. I want to bare my soul. To empty myself. To confess the whole business and finally be free.

(*He pauses and gathers his memories together*)

De Recha (*in a strangled voice*): Well?

Lefty: Fuck it. I can't. It's too terrifying.

(*He proceeds to garrote De Recha. De Recha, screaming and choking, paws at the ground and finds the gun he dropped. He points it at Lefty who tries to evade it, shots go off willy nilly, but both hands are busy, and in a terrible moment, De Recha blasts into Lefty who screams and dies. De Recha then puts the gun in his mouth and pulls*) *the trigger. After an interminable moment of silence, there is a knock at the door*)

De Recha (*getting up, with what's left of his voice*): Yes?

Voice: We got three crates here for 243 and a half Hope Street, is that you?

De Recha: Yes. I'll be right there. (*He goes over to the door, signs for the real crates and brings them into the room. Lefty seems to be coming back to life, though he is as confused as confused can be*) Nicely done old man, you did beautifully! *Very* nicely done. Things are going to work out just fine. Do you suppose you could give me a hand with these?

In and Out
of the
Light

by
Elaine May

The stage is divided into two rooms separated by a corridor that runs vertically between them. A slider panel conceals each room when it is not the focus of a scene.

The room R has a dentist's chair and equipment in it. The room L is Dr. Kesselman's private office. At the end of the corridor, U is a communications center built into the wall. Next to it is the glass-paneled door to the waiting room.

Dr. Kesselman is visible in his office lab, sitting behind the cluttered table, talking on the phone.

Dr. Kesselman: Dorrie, I'm sorry, honey, but I'm not going to be home for dinner again, I've got an emergency. A patient broke his dentures. . . . I don't know, maybe it's the lab, these last few weeks people are breaking crowns and bridges . . . I can't, he's flying to Paris in the morning. Well, darling, I can't ask him to fly to Paris without dentures and then try and find an English-speaking dentist on Saturday because you don't want me to miss dinner. . . . No, it's okay, I'll just grab a bite. The new assistant, Miss whaddayoucallit, is here. She'll order something for me. (*He laughs*) No, no, no. She's not a girl. She's *way* past being a girl. No, she's not attractive . . . big butt, rats nest hair, uniform doesn't fit. You'd send her right to the gym. Well, tell Harry I'll talk to him tomorrow, he can call me in the office. Dorrie, they have phones in dental school, don't make this . . .

(*He breaks off as a woman in a white nylon uniform comes in from the waiting room. She is what he has described but in a bizarrely sexual way. Her cleavage is visible over the top button of her uniform and huge breasts thrust against its taut fabric, revealing the shape of both nipples. Her waist is tiny, as if it has been cinched, and her hips swell out from underneath. Her legs in high heels originate from big, high, round buttocks, graphically outlined by her tight, short skirt. Her hair is very blonde, worn half up and half down, a la old Brigitte Bardot movies. Her make-up is bold, her lips full*)

Sue: Dr. Kesselman, Mr. Gilfoyle is asking about an appointment tomorrow. Shall I make one for him before I go home?

Dr. Kesselman: No, no, there's a Gay Pride parade in the morning and every patient will be thirty minutes late. Tell him to call the secretary on Monday. And then . . . (*Puts his hand over the mouthpiece*) if you can wait for five minutes. I'd like to ask you something.

(*She nods, then sways off into the waiting room*)

Dr. Kesselman: I have to hang up now, Dorrie. We have a little bleeding problem. Right . . . Love you, too.

(*He hangs up as Sue swivels back into the corridor*)

Dr. Kesselman: Sue, can you stay? I'd like to talk to you about . . . the new plastic curettes for implant scaling—among other things. I don't like them. I think they're too hard. What's your feeling?

Sue: Too "hard"?

Dr. Kesselman: Maybe I'm being finicky but it's just so damned important to maintain those implants. We spend all the money and time on implant research but when it comes to *maintaining* the damned things . . .

Sue: Oh, I know. That's so true of everything. Like they advertised these credit cards? And I called to order one and I spoke to someone who could barely speak English. And I never got one.

Dr. Kesselman (*after a moment, blankly*): Ah.

Sue: Like they must have spent so much on advertising they didn't have enough left to hire American citizens.

Dr. Kesselman: *Ah*! Yes. Perfect. Well, that's the point . . .

Sue: So what's the use of spending all that money? And sometimes they'll advertise clothes? Like designer clothes or shoes? And they'll never come out. They'll have just advertised them and never made them.

Dr. Kesselman: It's insane. It's just insane.

Sue: Except . . . this is like the fifth night in two weeks that I'll be staying late . . .

Dr. Kesselman: Oh, God. Well . . . you must be compensated. I didn't even realize. I'm going to see that overtime for all five nights, including any future nights, is included in your next check. Say time and a half?

Sue: Time and a half?

Dr. Kesselman: Double time? That seems fairer.

Sue: Oh, gee. That's so nice of you.

Dr. Kesselman: Not at all. You'll earn it . . . *have* earned it.

Sue: Thank you. The last dentist I worked for never paid me *any* overtime and he'd keep me late at least three times a week filing charts. He'd just sit there and *watch* me, you know, like he didn't think I could do it by myself. They were just the worst hours.

Dr. Kesselman: Terrible. Well, I know that a divorce leaves you strapped. You *are* divorced . . . ?

Sue: Yes. It leaves you strapped both financially and emotionally. Although I wasn't left, you know, just empty . . . like many women my age, because my career is fruitful.

Dr. Kesselman: You're much too young to be empty.

Sue: Well, I'm not . . . probably not as young as you think.

Dr. Kesselman: I hope not. I'd be arrested for being alone with you.

Sue (*laughing*): Oh, now ...

Dr. Kesselman: Seriously, I *do* know that the breakdown of a marriage is the most shattering thing that can happen to a person. Even if they don't get divorced. Especially if they don't.

Sue: Well, *I* think that if a marriage is breaking down a person should get out of it. Because if you stay in a bad relationship how can you look for a good one?

Dr. Kesselman: Yes. Wise words. Of course, children make it difficult ...

Sue: I think it's terrible for children to see their parents unhappy. I mean, even if they don't *see* arguments they always know somewhere. Something gives it away. Like my mother had a lot of lovers and she always pretended things were going great with them—but we always knew because her new guy would be giving it to me and my sister and my mom'd be talking about how great he was in bed ... and we *knew* that after he was done plowing *us* all night he wasn't going back and giving Mr. Happy a ride in Mom's tunnel but we always said "That's great, Mom" because we didn't want to hurt her feelings.

Dr. Kesselman (after a moment): Yes. Children are ... so sensitive.

Sue: Of course, I don't know what the circumstances are in the marriage you're talking about.

Dr. Kesselman: Well, just . . . sometimes a woman is a good woman but . . . I don't know. Maybe once she has everything, economically, I mean, the big house, the Lexus, the charge accounts, the interior decorators . . .

Sue: You're talking about, like, a rich woman . . .

Dr. Kesselman: Sue, I'm going to be frank with you. Because I think I can trust you. I'm talking about my wife.

Sue: Really. Dentists make that much?

Dr. Kesselman: A top reconstructive dentist who works the hours I've worked and charges the prices I've charged—oh, yes. Money. But without love . . . what does it all mean.

Sue: Yes. She has all the cars and the clothes and the beautiful children and the house and the money but what she's forgotten is that to make a marriage work it takes a man and a woman.

Dr. Kesselman: You know, if I could print that on every marriage certificate issued in this country it might go a long way to changing the divorce rate. That is *so* smart. Have you . . . do you write? Have you done any writing?

Sue: Not fiction. But I do try to write a letter to one magazine every week.

Dr. Kesselman: Very impressive. You know, this is so helpful talking this way. I don't know if it's been helpful for you . . .

Sue: Oh, yes. Because I'm a very private person, and that's made it difficult to talk about my marriage or divorce so I've never really had any closure.

Dr. Kesselman: Well, that's very dangerous . . . not to have closure. (*Groping*) Because . . . without closure . . .

Sue: . . . there's no healing.

Dr. Kesselman: Yes. Sue . . . is this nuts . . . to think we can help each other just by talking, maybe having an early dinner at, say, La Bernadin and just, I don't know, sharing our troubles? It's 5:30 so there won't be any problem with reservations.

Sue: Well . . . sometimes talking it out . . .

Dr. Kesselman: I'll make the reservation. (*He picks up the phone, dials, waits*) Why don't you change into your street clothes and then we can just . . . (*Into phone*) Ah. I'd like to make a reservation for two. For 6:15 . . .

(*Sue has gone out into the corridor, unbuttoning her smock as she goes. The phone rings in the corridor and she picks it up*)

Sue: Dr. Kesselman's office. He's on another line . . . Oh, my, hold on one minute, and I'll see if he's available.

Dr. Kesselman: . . . that will be fine. Kesselman. k-e-s-s-e-l-m-a-n. Thank you. (*He hangs up*)

Sue (*calling*): Dr. Kesselman. It's Ms. Perry on two.

Dr. Kesselman: Oh, shit. Did you tell her I was here?

Sue: Yes, but I said I'd see if you were available. She says she's in terrible pain . . .

Dr. Kesselman: Okay. (*She goes back out*)

Fuck! (*He picks up the phone*) Hi. What seems to be the trouble, Wanda? Uh-huh. Where is it? . . . Oh, that doesn't sound like much. Why don't I send you up some Demerol and you can come in tomorrow. I see . . . Where are you? . . . Yes, that *is* lucky. Right. See you in a minute. (*He hangs up*) Oh, God, this is a nightmare. She's so fucking phobic. I should never have taken her on as a patient. It's been fifteen years of hell.

Sue (*from the other room*): That's so unfair to *your* needs.

Dr. Kesselman: Well, she was young and terrified and I just moved my practice to Manhattan and I needed patients . . .

Sue: So, Dr. Kesselman . . . should I . . . I'll prepare the room and cancel La Bernadeen?

Dr. Kesselman: No. Don't cancel La Bernadin. It's only 5:30. Maybe it isn't serious and I can do it without novocaine. She says it's painful but a lot of that could be fear. I could use some water. (*He walks into the patient's cubicle*) Would you like a little water, Sue?

Sue: Well, perhaps a sippy. (*She squirts some water into a paper cup*)

Dr. Kesselman: So you have a sister. Is she a dental hygienist, too?

Sue: No. She's an actress. And dancer.

Dr. Kesselman: On Broadway?

Sue: No. She does movies. And she also performs live. (*Hands him the cup*)

Dr. Kesselman: I'm surprised you didn't go into show business, too. With your looks.

Sue (*squirts water into a second cup*): Well, I was in show business . . . but then one day I was at the dentist getting a cavity filled and he, the dentist, offered to put me through dental school.

Dr. Kesselman: You're joking. You mean, just like that. He didn't want anything from you?

Sue: Well, sex but I said no because I was married at the time. So then he said if I just went to work for him he could teach me to be a dental assistant, so I worked for him three years until he had a stroke.

Dr. Kesselman: What does . . . did your husband do?

Sue: Charlie was . . . kind of an agent. Before I learned dental assisting technique I had an act with my sister and another girl. And Charlie would book us into clubs and parties . . .

Dr. Kesselman (*clutching his cup*): Really? Too bad I didn't know you then. I . . . would like to have seen that act.

(*Harry, a young man, appears in the doorway*)

Harry: Dad?

Dr. Kesselman (*leaping up as if shot*): Harry, what are you doing here? This is Sue Delamar my new assistant we were just waiting for Ms. Perry she called with an emergency terrible pain she'll be here any minute I had another emergency a broken denture who was going to Paris but he canceled his trip so he'll probably come in tomorrow and now tonight I'll deal with this emergency Ms. Perry's emergency—

Sue: So you're Harry. Dr. Kesselman told me all about you. I thought you were much younger.

Harry: Well, I was.

Dr. Kesselman (*laughing very loudly*): Very good.

Sue (*blankly*): I don't understand.

Dr. Kesselman: Well, at one time he *was* much . . . younger . . . than he is now . . .

Sue: I thought he was, like, in high school.

Dr. Kesselman: No, no, no. Dental school.

Sue: I thought you said high school.

Dr. Kesselman: No, no, no. Dental school, going to be a dentist—like his grandpa and his old man. Right?

Harry: Uh . . . right. Mom said you were tied up with a patient so I thought . . .

Dr. Kesselman: I *am* tied up with a patient. I'm waiting for a patient right now. Ms. Perry, my patient . . .

Harry: . . . I thought . . . maybe when you're done with Ms. Perry we could have dinner . . . and talk.

Dr. Kesselman: Well . . . of course. Although I'll probably be exhausted after Ms. Perry.

Sue: So, Dr. Kesselman, should I put the broken denture in for tomorrow and cancel La Bernadeen?

Dr. Kesselman: What?

Sue: The broken denture who canceled Paris. The broken denture who was going to Paris tomorrow ...

Dr. Kesselman: OH! The broken denture. No. Yes. No. The secretary will do that tomorrow. Make a note for the secretary to put the broken denture in for tomorrow and change La Bernadeen to 8:30. Put her in right after La Perry. Thank you.

(*She goes out, frowning in bewilderment. Dr. Kesselman addresses Harry*)

Dr. Kesselman: La Bernadeen and La Perry in one night—what a pair of prima donnas, but you can't pick your emergencies.

Harry: Dad, you're not ...

Dr. Kesselman: Don't be insane. If I were going to fool around it would be with a young, slim, gorgeous girl not a dental assistant who looks like ... like ... like *her*.

Harry: I was going to say "you're not going to like this."

Dr. Kesselman: What?

Harry: You're not going to like what I have to say . . . the thing I want to talk to you about . . .

Dr. Kesselman: Oh. Yes. I was just . . . making a general . . .

(*A buzzer sounds again and again. Dr. Kesselman closes his eyes*)

Dr. Kesselman: It's her.

(*The door opens and Sue leads in a terrified Wanda Perry*)

Wanda: Oh, god oh god oh god oh god. Where's Carlotta? No, no, no, no. Dr. Kesselman! Where's Carlotta! I want Carlotta!

Dr. Kesselman: Carlotta went back to Puerto Rico, Wanda. This is my new assistant Sue . . .

Wanda: No! Oh, God! But does she know how to handle the nitrous? You can get brain damage from too much nitrous . . . no, no, no! What's that?

Dr. Kesselman: It's the chair. You've sat in this before. Just bend your knees, Wanda . . .

Wanda: Oh, God, oh God, oh God . . .

Harry: Hi, Ms. Perry.

Wanda: Who are you? How many people are going to be waiting on me . . . *working* on me at the same . . .

Harry: I'm Harry Kesselman, Ms. Perry.

Wanda: You're Harry? Harry with the levis and the zits. Oh, my God! I remember your bar mitzvah. Your father had to cancel my root canal. It was one of the happiest days of my life.

Harry: Did you ever get your dog to pee outside without putting a newspaper on the sidewalk?

Wanda: Oh! I'm going to cry! You remember Ginger. No. Never. He just couldn't grasp that there were two sets of rules for one act of nature. In that way he was very much like Einstein. What happened to your hamsters?

Harry: I had to give them away. They kept eating their young.

Wanda (*suddenly, as Sue tries to put the bib on her*): No! What are you doing? Oh, God! I don't think I can do this without Carlotta! Harry, I'm so scared.

Harry (*patting her hand*): I know. You'll be fine.

Wanda (*to Dr. Kesselman*): *You* put the bib on me.

Dr. Kesselman: I don't do that.

Wanda: Then let Harry do it.

Dr. Kesselman: All right. Harry, prep her.

Harry: What?

Sue (*from the doorway*): Maybe I should just go home.

Dr. Kesselman: No! Wait!

Sue: I mean, if she wants Carlotta and she wants Harry . . .

Dr. Kesselman (*to Harry*): Prep her fast. (*Hurrying after Sue*) Sue, wait! Let's . . . lets have some more water and talk about . . . we have to talk about . . . the implant curettes . . . Sue!

(*He is gone. Harry tries to turn the water on in the basin*)

Wanda: You know I'm nervous about the nitrous because it made me nervous last time. Usually it calms me—well, "calms" me is a little strong . . . but last time it just didn't work at all . . .

Harry (*the water shoots up, hitting him in the face*): Whoops.

Wanda: I'm hysterical. I fainted Sunday. I couldn't get straight what my accountant wanted me to do. He didn't have enough time to explain it to me. But after I fainted he gave me the whole afternoon and now I think I really have a hold of it. I have to list

every check. But that's just an example of how un-
stable I am—

(*Harry turns on some music*)

Wanda: I can't make your father understand that I
have panic attacks in life—so to go to the dentist is
very much like walking to my own execution ONLY
I'M NOT GUILTY . . . that music is making me *very*
anxious . . .

Harry: Sorry . . .

Wanda: . . . not that I *would* walk to my own execution. I'd be a raving psychotic by the time the priest
came.

Harry (*twiddling the knob*): Oh, *this* way is . . .

Wanda: *That's* what I don't understand about the
Catholics. If a priest comes to give you extreme
unction, you *know* you're dying. How do you keep
from just . . . blowing up with terror . . . just splat-
tering all over the walls . . . I better stop. Death . . .
death isn't a good . . . a good . . . anything. Oh, boy
oh boy oh boy oh boy.

Harry (*holding the bib*): Lift your hair.

Wanda: *OKAY!* Here it comes. Wait, wait, wait. Let
me turn on the tape recorder. I'm part of a panic
group. See what this is—I have this tape recorder.
When I'm entering a situation that gives rise to

panic I turn it on and then I say how scared I am at certain points . . . Like now when you're holding the bib!! Oh, my *God*!

Harry: You're scared of the bib?

Wanda: Terrified. The bib is about a five. (*Into recorder*) About a five. See, I rate it between 0 and 10. They give you a chart that tells how to do it but I was too anxious to read it.

Harry: Where is this group? I have panic attacks, too, and I've just been *looking* for something like this.

Wanda: You're kidding. You're just trying to soothe me. You have panic attacks? And you're a dentist?

Harry: Well, there's a question about that.

Wanda: What?

Harry: There's a question about whether I'm going to be a dentist.

Wanda: What's the question.

Harry (*he stares at her*): Whether I'm going to be a dentist. My father doesn't know yet, though—and I wondered if we could talk, like we did with the hamsters . . .

Wanda: . . . "with the hamsters" . . .

Harry: Remember I told you I was going into hamster farming instead of enrolling in college? When I was a kid? And you said "good choice." And I didn't even *know* you. You were just this patient of my dad's who was so crazy I knew I could tell you anything. And I was right. You were the only one who didn't think I was weird. But I didn't know they ate their young.

Wanda: Who?

Harry: The hamsters.

Wanda: Oh. Right. I'm sorry. Oh, Harry, I'm really sorry to be like this. And you're trying to tell me something.

Harry: Forgive me—but aren't you always like this?

Wanda: No. There are a few hours a day while I'm working when I'm actually a sentient human being.

Harry: Really? What do you do?

Wanda: I'm a psychologist. So you saw your hamsters eating their young. What a thing.

Harry: You're a *psychologist*?

Wanda: Why is that so surprising? Because I seem like an idiot in this chair? Everyone seems like an idiot somewhere. It just means you have imagination, you can see past the moment to the end, past the flesh to the skull. I can look at you right now and see your skull right through your forehead and that's how I know you'll be dead someday—and that means so will I—no, I won't. Yes, you will. No, I won't. Of course, you don't get much done with this kind of imagination . . . but too much gets done, anyway.

Harry (*after a moment*): You know . . . for a moment I couldn't follow you . . . and I got anxious because you sounded insane . . . but then, I realized that . . . *that's* what happened to me with the hamsters. It wasn't just that this mother hamster was eating her own children *while* they were climbing on her, trying to suckle, trusting her with their lives. It was that, suddenly, I saw the possibility of some blind eating *thing* just opening its jaws and sucking you in . . . like a breast getting even. Oh, it was traumatic. I think it's what made me gay.

Wanda: You're gay, too?

Harry: What do you mean "too"?

Wanda: I mean . . . I don't know what I mean.

Harry: That sounded . . . a little judgmental . . .

Wanda: No, no, no, I didn't mean it to be. I should be judgmental? I, who didn't have children because of the pain? I just mean wait until your father finds out you're not going to be a dentist and you're gay, too. Do you . . . have a friend?

Harry: Well . . . no, not really. I liked this one boy but he was Irish and his tongue was pierced . . . and he was very anti-semitic. I'm just so torn. I constantly dream that I'm hovering.

Wanda: The hovering dream, yes . . .

Harry: I can postpone telling dad about my career conflict for a while, but I *do* want to tell him I'm homosexual tonight—before the Gay Pride parade. What do you think?

Wanda: Smart call. Especially if you're going to march in it.

Harry: Oh, God no. Those awful costumes. And what if someone sees me? It's just . . . a symbolic deadline.

Wanda: Even better. Why don't you tell him right now. I can wait.

Harry: Now? Really? I'm just . . . so scared it will kill him. (*Punching his fist into the wall*) Oh, God, this is so hard. And I don't get anything out of it. I might as well be straight. I mean, to be gay and worry about your reputation and your father and your income and whether you should date a gentile—it's like being black without being cool. What's the fucking point?

Wanda: Yes. Well, being gay is your "idiot" area— and the dentist's chair is mine. But there's probably

also a place where you shine. We all go in and out of
the light.

Harry (*slowly*): "We all go in and out of the light."
What an interesting thing to say.

Wanda: And as for being afraid you'll kill your father—hey! One of the signs of maturity is the ability
to bear guilt.

Harry: Do you . . . do you have a card?

Wanda: Sure. Hand me my purse.

Harry (*handing it to her*): You know, it's amazing that
you understand so much and you're still so anxiety-
ridden. I mean . . . not to have children because
you're afraid of the pain. Do you ever regret it?

Wanda: Of course. Just as I regret not having friends
because I'm afraid they'll leave me. But it makes me
a better therapist—because there's no place I can't
go. Except . . . whoops. There's a place . . .

Harry: What?

Wanda: Nothing. I just thought of dying without children, aging . . . death . . . nothingness . . . oblivion
. . . (*Quickly into the tape recorder*) Nine . . . nine-
and-a-half . . . oh-oh . . .

Harry: You're okay.

Wanda: No! NO! ICE! I'M GOING OUT!

Harry: What? No! Wait!

(*He races out as Wanda lies moaning in the chair. He flings open his father's office door. Dr. Kesselman and Sue are now sipping Evian on ice. Kesselman leaps up*)

Harry: She wants ice. She's fainting.

Dr. Kesselman: Oh, shit.

(*Dr. Kesselman picks up his water and runs into Wanda's cubicle, followed by Sue*)

Wanda: Help, help, help, help, help, help . . .

Dr. Kesselman: You didn't even get the bib on her. Sue, raise the chair. Legs above hips.

Sue: Legs *above* hips?

(*Dr. Kesselman takes the ice from his glass and presses it on the back of Wanda's neck*)

Wanda: . . . help, help, help, help, help . . .

Dr. Kesselman: Take it easy, Wanda! You're okay.

(*The chair begins slowly rising to a sitting position*)

Dr. Kesselman: No, no, no, Sue! Head *down*. Feet up.

Sue: Oh. *I* see. *That* way above the hips . . .

(*Sue grabs Wanda's feet*)

Dr. Kesselman: No, no! Not *her* feet. The chair! Down! Down! All the way down!

Wanda: I'm going to faint.

Dr. Kesselman: You are not going to faint.

(*He throws his water in her face. She gasps . . . then . . .*)

Wanda (*weakly*): Thank you.

Dr. Kesselman: Why the hell didn't you take a tranquilizer before you came.

Wanda: I took three Valium. And two Percodan. The Percodan worked but the Valium acted like coffee. (*Into tape recorder*) That was a ten.

Dr. Kesselman: Better? (*Wanda nods*) Sue, prepare the nitrous . . .

Wanda: No! Not her!

Dr. Kesselman: Wanda, I can't work on you without an assistant. I need suction, I need . . .

Wanda: Yes, yes, I know, but . . . please, not the nitrous. I don't know her. Please, please, I don't want her in here until after the nitrous . . . (*To Sue*) No offense. (*To Dr. Kesselman*) Please!

Dr. Kesselman (*he takes a deep breath*): Alright, wait outside until the nitrous takes effect, will you, Sue?

(*Sue walks slowly out of the cubicle and into Dr. Kesselman's office—where Harry sits with his head in his hands. Behind her Dr. Kesselman picks up the nitrous mask*)

Wanda: Wait, wait, wait, wait . . . I don't want the mask yet! Wait! Oh, God, Oh God! There's nothing coming out of it. I'm sucking rubber!

Dr. Kesselman: I haven't turned it on yet.

Wanda: Wait!

(*Dr. Kesselman closes the door behind him*)

Harry: Is she all right?

Sue: Yes. He's giving her nitrous.

Harry: Man, that . . . that was harrowing.

Sue: "Harrowing?"

Harry: Just to see someone come unglued like that . . .

Sue: Yes, it's very nerve-wracking. I made a lot of mistakes in there, but I got so mixed up . . .

Harry: And what can you do. She's a patient and she's scared . . . and you're scared . . .

Sue: I mean when he started barking orders at me it just reminded me of every time my stepfather yelled you're squeezing it too hard . . . you're hurting it . . . you're this! . . . you're that! It made me feel so stupid.

Harry: Well, there . . . there's always some place in life where you seem like an idiot. And some place where you shine.

(*Dr. Kesselman appears upstage center and turns a valve*)

Sue: "Some place where you shine . . ."

Wanda (*calling*): What are you doing?

Dr. Kesselman (*calling back*): I'm turning the nitrous valve on.

(*He goes quickly into the lab room where Sue sits with Harry*)

Dr. Kesselman: Sue, why don't you . . . check the . . . sort the . . . switch the . . . put the . . . unwrap the implant curettes. I'll be ready in a few minutes. Harry, after the patients leave Sue and I have to go over the implant curettes so why don't you . . .

Wanda: It's too high! I'm getting dizzy. Turn it down! It's too HIGH!

Dr. Kesselman (*shouting back*): Shut up! I'm coming. GodDAMit.

(*He goes out*)

Sue: He keeps asking me about the implant curettes. And I don't know what to say. I'm not a hygienist. He's going to think I'm a moron.

Harry: Why doesn't he ask *me* about the implant curettes. I could tell him. Oral hygiene is where I shine. God, I could save so many people so much time and so much money. But in dentistry if you're not *the* guy who makes the diagnosis, *the* guy who makes the cut, you're no one. Try saying you're interested in oral nursing or oral hygiene to someone like my father and he'll say, "Why? Can't you make it as a dentist?"

Sue: Yes. I could have been a hygienist. But it would have meant having sex with my dentist.

Harry: That's a tough call.

Sue (*vaguely*): Yes. But I was married.

Harry: I mean . . . I *love* dental hygiene, it's like teaching. And being a dentist is so high pressure, it just eats up your life—we never saw my father—but I'm also aware that there are a lot more perks for a dentist than a hygienist.

Sue: Maybe not. Who's to say? Who's to say what "perks" are? May I read you this letter I cut out of *People* magazine? (*She picks up a magazine*) "Bill Gates may enjoy working full time to make his billions now but when he is dying I doubt he'll say 'I wish I'd spent more time on my career.' "

Harry: I . . . I'm not sure what you're saying.

Sue (*reading*): "Bill Gates may enjoy . . ."

Harry: No, no, no. I understand the letter, I mean . . . I'm not sure how it relates to me . . . or what the point of it is. Bill Gates will probably only be dying for a couple of weeks and he'll have enjoyed himself for sixty years.

Sue: But who's to say? Who's to say he wouldn't trade those sixty years of perks for a rich and loving last few weeks. I mean when I didn't go to bed with my dentist I had doubts. I mean, I'd gone to bed with so many guys just because I was hot or it was too much trouble not to, and then when I had a chance to get an education out of it I didn't, and my husband left me anyway. Sure I have a profession— which is more than my sister has, and I really worry about that because when her boobs drop it's over—but it's not a *real* profession like I could have had if I'd let Dr. Schleiman pump me. And you know what I finally decided? (*Harry shakes his head, mutely*) Who's to say? Who's to say I'd've been as happy as a hygienist? Who's to say trying to be a good wife and working on the act so Charlie could book us and get off watching us wasn't the right thing to do? If I thought it was the right thing to do I must've been getting off, too, so who's to say that nursing people and saving their teeth and getting off with someone you think is hot doesn't make up for all the perks you get as a dentist.

Harry (*after a moment*): Well, you've . . . made some very good putz . . . *points* . . . very good *points* . . . but "getting off," as you say, isn't everything . . .

Sue: It is while you're doing it.

Harry: But what about when you're not.

Sue: I try not to have too much down time.

Harry: I see. Well . . . thank you for your advice but it's a moot point because I'm . . . I'm a bit . . . uh . . . "monkish" when it comes to sex . . . so a life of "getting off" is not a real option.

Sue: Would you like me to introduce you to someone? I know some really cute guys.

Harry: Some *what*! What are you talking about! Do you think I'm *gay*? Well, you must. But . . . but . . . but *why*? Why would you think that?

Sue (*she pats his cheek*): Oh . . . just because the nice ones always are. This one guy I know—I think you'd really like him—his teeth aren't great and he's short but he has a dong that could dust streetlights. (*He stares at her*) It's just an expression.

Harry: No, it isn't. I've never heard that expression.

Sue: Really? Then maybe it's the title of something.

Harry: I'm getting very anxious.

Sue: I'm sorry, but I can't introduce you tonight. I'm having dinner with your father at La Bernadeen. How about tomorrow night?

Harry: No, no. I'm not getting *that* kind of anxious . . . "La Bernadeen"? La Bernadeen is . . . isn't La Bernadeen your patient?"

Sue: You mean the whole restaurant?

Harry: No. I mean . . . you mean . . . what do you mean? You mean La Bernadin . . . is a restaurant. The restaurant La Bernadin! Where you're having dinner . . . with my father. Tonight.

(*Harry suddenly turns and marches out the door . . . and flings open the door of the patient's cubicle. Dr. Kesselman is dozing. Wanda, now wearing the nitrous mask, opens her eyes*)

Wanda (*from under the mask*): Wha . . . !

Dr. Kesselman: Where . . . ! (*He sees Harry*) Goddamit, Harry . . . she was almost under.

Harry: I just came to tell you that if you can't talk to me now I'll just hang around and assist you with your 8:30 patient, you can let Sue go home.

Dr. Kesselman: What? No! No, no. I . . . It . . . It's silly to hang around . . . In fact, if I finish with Wanda early enough I may just call La Bernadeen and send her over to Dr. Blumenthal. It sounds like it's a "gum" thing anyway and I'm so exhausted I'll probably just leave . . .

Harry: Well, let's wait and see what happens. How're you doing, Wanda?

Wanda: Oh, God.

Harry: Uh-huh. Call me if you need me, Dad.

(*He walks out of the cubicle, back into the office, opens a drawer and takes out a pint bottle of liquor as the glider closes*)

Dr. Kesselman: Shit.

Wanda: It's root canal, isn't it?

Dr. Kesselman: How the hell would I know. You won't let me see the tooth.

Wanda: Because the last time I was here I felt the novocaine shot.

Dr. Kesselman: That was the interligementus injection but I won't use the interligmeject today.

Wanda: How do you know if you haven't seen my tooth?

Dr. Kesselman: Wanda, I refuse to continue this discussion. Open your mouth.

Wanda: But I don't feel anything from the nitrous. I'm not ready. I'm not ready, I'm not ready, I'm not ready!

Dr. Kesselman: Yes, you are. You're higher than a kite.

Wanda: No, I'm not.

Dr. Kesselman: Yes, you are.

Wanda: No, I'm not. I'm not. I'm not. I'm not. Why are you treating me like this? As if I were a normal person. You know what I'm like, you know how long it takes me. I'll pay you extra if I'm wasting your time. I was one of three patients when you first moved here. I used to pay in advance so you could meet the rent . . .

Dr. Kesselman: Alright, alright, alright.

Wanda: I can't just open my mouth. I have to be ready . . .

Dr. Kesselman: Alright. I said alright!

Wanda: I know. But I need so much reassurance. That's why I lose everyone. It's not the needle. I don't care about the penetration. I understand that my fear is all a rape fantasy but it's complicated because I'm ambivalent about being raped so I get angry at anyone I fantasize raping me. And then I get frightened of being angry because I'm afraid it will antagonize my rapist.

Dr. Kesselman: Wanda, you're babbling.

Wanda: I know. Please don't be angry. I'm so petrified.

Dr. Kesselman: Stop saying that. You're just rein-
forcing it.

Wanda: But don't you want to know how I feel?

Dr. Kesselman: No. I want you to open your mouth
so I can look at your tooth and give you a topical before the Percodan wears off—

Wanda: Oh, God. Oh God, oh God, okay. Okay, okay.
Okay. Okay. But I don't know what to think about.
Tell me something to think about.

Dr. Kesselman: Open up.

Wanda: I'm going to count backwards by sevens.

Dr. Kesselman: Good idea. Where is it? Oh, I see . . .

Wanda: Oh, God! Is it something awful? Don't tell
me! 100 . . . 93 . . . 86 . . . 86 . . .

Sue (*who has wandered to the doorway*): 87, 88 . . .

Dr. Kesselman: No, no, you idiot. She's counting
backwards by sevens. (*Sue slinks away*) No! SUE!
Oh, *shit*!

(*Dr. Kesselman rushes out of the room and grabs Sue in the corridor*)

Wanda: Larry? LARRY!

Dr. Kesselman (*calling*): I'll be right back. Sue, I'm sorry. She just . . . drove me insane. I didn't know what I was saying.

Wanda: LARRY!

Dr. Kesselman: Yes!

Sue: I think I should go home now. It's getting pretty late and I've made so many mistakes . . .

Dr. Kesselman: No, no, no. You've made no mistakes . . .

Wanda (*calling*): Larry, you didn't give me the topical.

Dr. Kesselman: Alright! I coming! (*To Sue*) Please. Please don't go home. This won't take long, I promise.

(*Sue walks slowly back into the office where Harry sits drinking, and the gliders close. Dr. Kesselman rushes back into the patient's cubicle and dips a cotton swab into a bottle of gel*)

Wanda: What's that?

Dr. Kesselman: Open your mouth.

Wanda: Okay, but wait, but wait, wait, wait . . .

Dr. Kesselman: No. You said you wanted the topical.

Wanda: I said you didn't give it to me yet. Larry, I'm sweating with panic.

Dr. Kesselman: I don't care.

Wanda: Oh, God! You're angry! I'm going to faint.

Dr. Kesselman: Wanda, I want you to do something for me.

Wanda: What is it?

Dr. Kesselman: I want you to help me get out of here by 8:30.

Wanda: Why? What's happening at 8:30?

Dr. Kesselman: At 8:30—if I live—I'm going to try to do something I've never done. In my entire life.

Wanda: What?

Dr. Kesselman: This thing.

Wanda: What thing? It's not . . . suicide, is it?

Dr. Kesselman: Suicide? Why would you say that?

Wanda: I don't know. You're just . . . acting so strange. Have you talked to Harry?

Dr. Kesselman: About what?

Wanda: About . . . about what he wants to talk to you about.

Dr. Kesselman: No. I'll do that tomorrow. Tonight I want to do *this*.

Wanda: *What?*

Dr. Kesselman: This *thing*. (*He shoves the cotton swab with the topical into her mouth*) This . . . careless, mindless, goyish . . . thing. And I'm asking for your help.

Wanda: What kind of careless, mindless boyish thing?

Dr. Kesselman: Goyish—not boyish. Well, maybe they're both the same to me.

Wanda: What kind of goyish thing? Drinking? Parachute diving?

Dr. Kesselman: Better.

Wanda: You mean worse?

Dr. Kesselman: Yes.

(*He dips another cotton swab in the gel*)

Wanda: Is it . . . a crime? The thing you're going to do?

Dr. Kesselman: Almost. But no one will be hurt. That's what makes it goyish. (*Shoving the second cotton swab in her mouth*)

Wanda: I'm getting very nervous. For you, I mean. Why would you suddenly want to do this thing at 8:30 tonight?

Dr. Kesselman: Because I can. Because circumstances have made it available to me. Because tonight I feel like somebody called Dino and by tomorrow I won't. Do you know what they called me in junior high school? "Dr. Kesselman." In junior high—"Hey, Dr. Kesselman, catch the ball!" I was terrible at sports, I didn't date shiksas, I brought an extra sweater to school just in case, I didn't go swimming until an hour after I ate and I was hungry all the time so I spent all day at the beach checking my watch. And now I'm grown and my life is exactly the same except that my father calls me Ada because he thinks I'm my mother, and my sister has an ovarian cyst, and my wife spends all her time at the gym fighting osteoporosis . . .

Wanda: Does it have something to do with sex?

Dr. Kesselman: What?

Wanda: This thing you want me to help you do?

Dr. Kesselman: Uh . . . yes. But it's not just sex. It's porno sex.

Wanda: Is it something to do with that refugee from channel 35?

Dr. Kesselman: Who?

Wanda: Your assistant.

Dr. Kesselman: Uh . . .

Wanda: If it is . . . I just want to say . . . if you're looking for something more out of life . . . don't look for it in the gutter.

(*He dips a third cotton swab in the bottle*)

Dr. Kesselman: I'm not looking for something more out of life. I'm looking for something less. Something cheap. Something easy.

(*He shoves the third cotton swab in her mouth*)

Wanda: Is that why you were never attracted to me?

Dr. Kesselman: What?

Wanda: Were you ever attracted to me?

Dr. Kesselman: You? Are you serious? You're too much trouble to . . . to even think about let alone have a fantasy over.

Wanda: Sometimes love is worth the trouble.

Dr. Kesselman: I'm not interested in love. I'm interested in sex. Love means you have to do a lot of work to keep from hurting someone. And then they get hurt anyway because they love you. Sex means a good time . . .

Wanda: Your son is gay.

Dr. Kesselman: *What!*

Wanda: I'm sorry. He was going to tell you anyway.

Dr. Kesselman: Oh, my *God!*

Wanda: So, now is no time to be having porn sex. Oh, good! I'm numb.

Dr. Kesselman (*running into the corridor*): Harry!

(*Harry runs out of the office. Sue follows*)

Dr. Kesselman: You're GAY?

Harry: Well . . . you were going to La Bernadin with *Sue.*

Dr. Kesselman: What the hell has that got to do with being gay!

Harry: Just . . . everybody's sexual tastes . . . (*Shouting at Wanda*) Thanks a *lot!* (*To Dr. Kesselman*) Dad, please don't be mad at me.

Dr. Kesselman: Do you know how hard it is for a gay dentist to get straight patients?

Sue: He doesn't want to be a dentist. He wants to be a hygienist.

(*Dr. Kesselman staggers. Harry rushes to him*)

Dr. Kesselman: No, no. I'm alright. (*He straightens*) How can you be gay? Aren't you dating this . . . that girl . . . some girl . . .

Harry: Yes, but it's just a cover. She's gay, too.

Dr. Kesselman: She's gay? Too? But . . . what . . . AIDS . . .

Harry (*bitterly*): Don't worry. No virus can get past my two condoms and my exhaustive inquiry into the medical history of my date. I can barely get laid.

Dr. Kesselman: Excuse me.

(*He goes into his office and shuts the door*)

Harry (*turning on Wanda*): Why? Why did you do this to me? Why did you tell him this way?

(*There is a thud from the office. Sue screams. Harry freezes*)

Harry: Oh, my God! DAD! (*He rushes forward and flings open the office door. Dr. Kesselman is lying on the floor. Harry races to him, kneels, takes his pulse, then calls to Sue*) Call 911. (*Sue hurries to the com-*

munications center U . . . past Wanda, who staggers into the office, the cotton swab still in her mouth. Dr. Kesselman's eyes open) Dad . . .

Dr. Kesselman: What was the big thing . . . she's older, she wouldn't have expected a lot, she would've been happy with overtime and half her rent paid, she would have been worry-free . . . low maintenance . . .

Wanda: Are you talking about Sue? And what if in a year she got breast cancer or an ovarian cyst. Would you drop her? No. You'd have to take care of her. She'd be another burden.

Dr. Kesselman (*to Harry*): Make her go away.

Harry: I . . . I'll try. (*Shouting*) Sue! Sue! (*Sue sticks her head in*) Tell them they've got to hurry.

Sue: They haven't picked up yet.

Harry: Well, do something! He's dying!

Wanda (*clapping her hands over her ears*): Don't say "dying."

Harry: HELP! Dad! Please!

(*Dr. Kesselman opens his eyes*)

Harry: Dad . . . Dad . . .

Dr. Kesselman: Your mother was . . . wonderful about my not being there . . .

Harry: Yes. She's like that, isn't she?

Dr. Kesselman: I don't know what she's like. I wasn't there.

Harry: Just relax. You were great. *Are* great. How do you feel?

Dr. Kesselman: Better. Much better. I got dizzy . . .

Harry: Good. You're getting some color back. You know, Wanda . . . Wanda went way over the top just now . . .

(*Wanda suddenly gasps—then doubles over*)

Harry: What? I just said you went over the top. That's not so . . .

Wanda: The Percodan . . . wore off . . . and the nitrous . . .

Dr. Kesselman: And the topical?

Wanda (*she nods*): Oh, the *pain*! The PAIN!

Dr. Kesselman: Harry, give her a novocaine shot.

Harry: *What?*

Wanda: Help! (*Into recorder*) Five.

Dr. Kesselman: Give her a novocaine shot. It sounds like a nerve.

Wanda (*hands over ears*): I don't want to hear that.

Harry (*to his father*): I can't leave you.

Dr. Kesselman: No, no, leave me. I'll be alright. But I'm not up to the shot. Harry don't let her suffer. She's been my patient for fifteen years. Sue, call Blumenthal and ask him how fast he can get here from Long Island. Harry, *go*.

Harry: Oh, my God. (*He rises, trembling, and takes the groaning Wanda's arm*) Sue, don't leave my father. Tell me at the first sign of any change, call me as soon as the paramedics get here . . .

Wanda: Oh god, oh god, oh god, oh god . . .

Harry: Oh god, oh god . . .

(*He leads Wonds out, his groans and the groans of Wonda and Dr. Kesselman joining in a harsh corus of pain . . . until the gliders close on the office L.*)

Harry (*leading her into the cubicle*): Oh god, oh god . . . please . . . this is my first time with an actual patient, so . . . (*helping her into the chair*) . . . be kind.

Wanda: Oh, help! Help! Wait, wait, wait, wait. Harry, now when you shoot the novocaine in, doesn't it shoot ahead of the needle? So, if you do it very, very, very slow . . .

Harry: Yes, yes. Very slow.

Wanda: But first more topical.

Harry: Yes.

(*Harry begins putting on a mask*)

Wanda: Why are you putting on a mask?

Harry: That's how we do it in school. Please don't mix me up. I'm so frightened.

Wanda (*into tape recorder*): Thirty.

Harry: You'll be fine. Put this topical on your gum. (*She takes the cotton swab and puts it in her mouth. Harry calls*) How're you doing, Dad?

Sue (*calling back*): He's on with Dr. Blumenthal.

(*Harry picks up the syringe from the cabinet*)

Wanda: Oh, God! I see what you're doing. I'm not ready.

Harry: I'm just going to hold it in my hand until the topical works.

Wanda: That's not a ligmaject is it?

Harry: No.

Wanda: Why is it different from the ligmaject? Or is it? Oh, my God! It *isn't*! You're going to use the ligmaject, aren't you?

Harry: No, no. I'm not. Why would I use a ligmaject? *Should* I use a ligmaject?

Wanda: No, No!

Harry: I don't know what I'm doing!

Wanda: Alright, alright. Don't get hysterical. (*Into tape recorder*) Twenty-eight and steady. Now, Harry . . .

Harry: Please don't make me any more nervous than I am. Just breathe. Don't talk! Alright, the topical should've worked by now . . .

Wanda: Oh, no! I'm not ready. I'm not ready, I'm not ready, I'm not ready!

Harry: Okay. Maybe we should wait.

Wanda: Are you crazy? I have nerve involvement. That tooth could blow up and kill me.

Harry: Well, what do I do? How does my father do it? I don't know how to get someone to do something they don't want to do. That's why I'm not a dentist. What do I *do*?

Wanda: Shut up and I'll tell you. Alright, now touch the needle to my gum. But just touch it. Right?

Harry: Yes, yes.

Wanda: Just wait, just wait. Okay. Go ahead. OH, GOD! Ow, ow, ow, ow, ow.

Harry: I haven't done anything yet.

Wanda: I know but take it away. Take it away, take it away, take it away, take it away. Oh. Phew. See, now, that wasn't bad you idiot. Okay. How much worse will it be now?

Harry: I don't know. I was going to ask you that.

Wanda: No, no. Don't ask me anything—Just tell me it won't hurt and then pull my cheek like this . . . (*She pulls his cheek*) . . . while you give it to me.

Harry: Okay. Oh, God. Now, Wanda, this won't hurt . . .

Wanda: . . . I'm going to give you a few drops, pull the needle out, a few more drops, needle out . . . just like I always do . . .

Harry: . . . few drops needle out, few more drops, needle out . . . until we're very, very old . . . while I pull your cheek like this . . . (*He pulls her cheek*) . . . just like I always do . . . and then it will be over.

Wanda: Oh, God. Oh God, oh God, okay. Okay, okay. Oh God—you look like you're getting so ready . . .

Harry: Stop talking or I won't be able to do it.

Wanda: Yes, you will. I can talk without moving my head. Oh, I'm petrified. Yes, I am. Harry, pull my cheek harder. Ow. Slower, ow, slower.

Harry: Will you shut up so I can get your lip?

Wanda: 86—79—72—Ow! Ow! Ow!

Harry: Please don't move. Please, please . . .

Wanda: Ow, please . . .

Harry: Oh, please . . .

Wanda: Oh, please! Take it out, take it out. Please— ow—please, please, please, please. . . . Take it out. Take it out.

Harry: It's out.

Wanda: Did you get it all in?

Harry: You told me not to.

Wanda: Oh, shit.

Harry: But I did anyway.

Wanda: You're kidding. You gave me the whole shot. I'm done with the novocaine?

Harry: Yes.

Wanda: You swear to God!

(*He shows her the empty syringe*)

Wanda: Un-fucking-believable! You're amazing.

Harry: Not bad for a gay dentist.

Wanda: Awesome! Un-fucking-credible. You don't know how incredible! (*She throws her arms around him*) Oh, Harry, thank you. That was amazing! Thank you! God bless you.

Harry: Dad! Dad! (*He runs out of the cubicle*) *I* gave Wanda her novocaine shot.

Wanda (*following him*): He was masterful, Larry. He did it in three minutes. He beat your record by an hour and a half.

Dr. Kesselman: Good ... that's good ... (*He closes his eyes*) That's good.

Harry: Dad? (*To Sue*) What happened?

Sue: 911 answered and I gave them the address. And then Dr. Kesselman hung up on Dr. Blumenthal and said "Oh, God, don't let the midtown tunnel be blocked" and then he sort of ... drifted off.

Harry: Dad? (*Kneeling beside him*) You know what else, Dad? I decided I *am* going to be a dentist, I *want* to be a dentist. I'm going to be a gay dentist but ... hey, I won't even be gay if you don't like it.

(*Dr. Kesselman pats his sons hand. A small, subtle light comes up on him as he speaks*)

Dr. Kesselman: No . . . be gay . . . if you want, Harry. One day . . . you'll have a heart attack . . . and it won't matter what you were two minutes before . . . it will just matter what you are two minutes from when you had the heart attack . . . do you think I'm going to die?

Harry: No! No!

Wanda (*struggling with panic, then firmly*): A'solu'ely not. You not goee to "die," Larry. Don't be afraid.

Dr. Kesselman (*gently*): My first . . . little patient in New York . . . my little Wanda . . .

(*Wanda presses her forehead against his hand and bursts into tears*)

Wanda: Oh, Larry . . . you ha such a goo heart an I gimmen you so much trouble . . .

Dr. Kesselman: No . . . Life gave me trouble . . . marriage . . . it was probably my fault but it was so unpleasant . . . I was thinking just now . . . I'll have to stay home with Dorrie if it's a heart attack. No extreme measures in the hospital, please . . . . I don't want to be hooked up to things . . . (*His eyes close*)

Harry: Dad, you don't have to go home. You can go wherever you want.

Dr. Kesselman: I don't even know where that would be, Harry.

Sue: Dr. Kesselman? So shall I cancel tomorrow?

Dr. Kesselman: Oh, yes . . . no more tomorrows. I wish . . . I could have seen your act, Sue.

Sue: Well . . . as soon as you feel better I'll call Norma and my sister and we'll do it for you.

Dr. Kesselman: Norma?

Sue: My sister's friend. I still have all our costumes. They're in my other purse.

Dr. Kesselman: Really . . .

Sue: Uh-huh. We wore little white caps and aprons and stockings with very high heels.

Dr. Kesselman: What held up the stockings?

Sue: Garters. And our aprons came to about here . . . (*she points to her crotch*) . . . and tied in back, and we carried little feather dusters, and we would lift our feather dusters and step into the light . . .

(*As she speaks a light comes up on her and the music begins. She lifts her arms*)

Sue: . . . and then we would raise our hands over our heads and pretend we were dusting the ceiling . . .

(*she turns around and bends over*) . . . and then we would bend down and pretend we were dusting the floor, and then we would sing . . . (*she begins dancing to the music, the dance she did in her act*)
"Twist those dusters,
Roll those hips,
Shake your booty,
Wet your lips . . .
We mean business,
We're open for business."

Dr. Kesselman: Pretty song.

Wanda: Isn't it?

Harry: I love it.

(*As she sings Dr. Kesselman takes a bottle of Bufferin from the table and begins feebly shaking it to the music. Harry and Wanda look at him with sudden hope . . . Harry grabs the liquor bottle from the table and begins tapping it with the empty novocaine needle. Wanda picks up the hinged display dentures and begins clicking them like marachas. Sue sings on*)

Sue: "Meet my sister,
And my sister's friend
If you lay us end to end,
We mean business,
We're open for business . . ."

Harry: And you know what else, Dad? Sue's going to introduce me to her friend, maybe we can . . . double date.

Wanda: Maybe we can triple date. (*To Sue*) Do you have someone for me?

Sue: Sure. (*Singing*)
"I like Norma, she likes me, too,
She likes my sister,
And we all like you,
We mean . . ."

(*She points to Dr. Kesselman*)

Dr. Kesselman (*singing*): ". . . business" . . .

Sue: "We're open for . . ."

Dr. Kesselman (*struggling to rise*): ". . . business . . ."

Sue: "We gotta have . . ."

Harry and Wanda: ". . . business . . ."

Sue: ". . . We'll give you the . . ."

All: "business" . . .

(*Dr. Kesselman, supported by Harry and Wanda, has now risen. Sue takes his hand and leads him center-stage*)

Sue: "We'll polish our knockers,
We'll shake off our dust,
We'll take out your tools,

And we'll strip off your rust,
We mean . . ."

Dr. Kesselman: ". . . business . . ."

(*They are now all standing, looking at Dr. Kesselman*)

Sue: "We mean . . ."

All: ". . . business . . ."

(*Dr. Kesselman totters, then straightens—then all four turn to the audience and begin stepping in sync . . . singing toward some distant point*)

All: "Twist those dusters,
   Roll those hips,
   Shake your booty,
   Wet your lips . . .
   We mean business,
   We're open for business . . ."

(*They continue to sing and move as the lights fade out.*)